A Surgeon's Century

The Life of
Sir Ian Fraser DSO FRCS

Penicillin team 1943 in Algiers, with Ian Fraser in front row.

A Surgeon's Century

The Life of
Sir Ian Fraser DSO FRCS

by
Richard Clarke

ULSTER HISTORICAL
FOUNDATION

First published in 2004
by Ulster Historical Foundation
12 College Square East, Belfast, BT1 6DD
www.ancestryireland.com
www.booksireland.org.uk

ISBN 1 903688 50 7

Design by CheahDesign
Printed by ColourBooks Ltd, Dublin

Contents

List of Illustrations

Frontispiece – Penicillin team 1943, in Algiers

1.   Dr Robert Moore Fraser (1865–1952)

2.   Dr Alexander Cuthbert (1834–1876)

3.   RBAI Under–XV Rugby Team 1915–6

4.   Resident medical staff, Royal Victoria Hospital, 1923–4

5 a Piece of glass removed from hand 1933
  b Brigadier Ian Fraser, Mark, Mary Alice and Eleanor 1945

6 a Party at Royal Victoria Hospital to celebrate Ian's receiving a
     knighthood 1963
  b Armorial bookplate 1969

7 a Award of Honorary MRCPI 1977
  b Award of Honorary FRCSI to Loyal Davis 1981

8.   Family group 1982

9 a Unveiling of memorial plaque in Ward 18 in 1992 in honour
     of the Working Men's Committee
  b Award of Honorary LlD from QUB 1992

10. Unveiling of Carol Graham's portrait of Sir Ian Fraser 1994

Foreword

On 14th July 1981 in the Ambassador's Residence at the Irish Embassy in Washington D.C. and in the presence of President and Mrs Reagan and Mrs Reagan's mother, Edith Davis, an Honorary Fellowship of the Royal College of Surgeons in Ireland was conferred on the neuro-surgeon, Loyal Davis, father of the First Lady. The citation had been entrusted to the 80-year-old Sir Ian Fraser, the accepted doyen of Irish surgeons. 'Dr Davis', he said, 'it is interesting to see that one man can be an editor, a teacher, an administrator, a surgeon and a soldier – such is given to very few'. Rembrandt never painted so faithful a self-portrait since with these words Sir Ian could have been painting himself.

Ian Fraser's long life (he died on 11th May 1999 in his 99th year) was one of uninterrupted success the more unusual since it covered a period of great changes in surgical practice and procedures and in the structure and administration of the profession. An outstanding undergraduate career, unequalled at Queen's for over 30 years, first place in both parts of the Fellowship of the Irish College of Surgeons, many other distinctions not all within the profession, and a publication record which, unusual for a surgeon, earned him an early (aged 38) Fellowship of the Royal Society of Edinburgh, evidenced an exceptional talent and heralded a note-worthy career. Outstanding war service (he became a much-decorated Brigadier) temporarily interrupted his smooth ascent to the pinacle of Ulster surgery which he ultimately reached and where he remained, in shared possession, until his final retirement.

Into this long life Ian packed ten life-times' activities and all pursued seemingly effortlessly and without ruffling his unfailing composure and that infectious charm, humour and congeniality which delighted all who met him. As was said of a distinguished predecessor, Sir Thomas Myles, 'He was at home with the highest as the lowest were at home with him'. Ian simply bubbled with vivaciousness and brio; he never seemed despondent still less morose.

The title of his autobiographical memoir *Blood, Sweat and Cheers* (1989) and its penultimate sentence "I have had one of the happiest lives that any man could wish for [and] a very happy home life entirely due to my wife and our two children" epitomise his life's journey and his sense of values.

I have long held with my Ulster colleagues that Ian deserves a biographer: indeed I said as much in my panegyric at his funeral[1]. With characteristic enthusiasm Emeritus Professor Richard Clarke accepted the family's invitation. He is admirably suited to the task. Honorary Archivist at the Royal Victoria Hospital Belfast and author of its aclaimed bicentenary history[2] and much else besides, he is as well-known in Irish historical and associated circles as he is in international anaesthesiology ones. He was assisted in every way by the Fraser family especially Ian's son Mark, himself a doctor and qualified surgeon who supplemented the existing sources with much additional personal information and unpublished material. The finished product is comprehensive, sympathetic but not hagiological, objective and measured in argument and opinion and is a worthy biography of an outstanding Ulsterman who found success in several fields and deserved his status of legend in his lifetime.

When Laurence Sterne portrayed his larger-than-life father in *Tristram Shandy*, he needed to create two characters, Walter Shandy and Uncle Toby; the real man was too much for one. Biographers of Ian face the same problem but with the added doubt as to whether two characters would be enough! The author fluently surmounts these hurdles in this perceptive and readable book which not just Irish doctors but many others will wish to have on their bookshelves whether or not they follow the avocations which Ian mirrored in his citation, already noted, honouring Dr Loyal Davis, Nancy Regan's father, in Washington in 1981.

PETER FROGGATT
BELFAST

1   Froggatt, P. 'Sir Ian Fraser 1901–1999'. *Ulster Medical Journal* 1999; 68: 49–53.
2   Clarke, R.S.J. *The Royal Victoria Hospital Belfast: A History* 1797–1997. Belfast, 1997.

Introduction and Acknowledgements

This biography of Sir Ian Fraser was undertaken at the request of his son Mark and has the advantage (and disadvantage) that I was taught by its subject over fifty years ago and came into frequent contact with him since then in The Royal Victoria Hospital. Memories and reputations fade quickly and now that Sir Ian has been dead for five years it seemed important to record as much as possible of his long and interesting life, from family records, conversation with colleagues and my own direct knowledge. Sir Ian wrote his autobiography in 1989 but it gives a very personal and anecdotal picture of his life. I have tried here to include more factual detail of his family and early history and of his later involvement with public bodies – particularly with the BMA and Royal College of Surgeons in Ireland.

I have been fortunate that the family has given me access to all the personal papers, diaries, newspaper cuttings and photographs collected by Sir Ian during his career and I am very grateful to Mark and Mary Alice for their help throughout the writing. I am grateful to the BMA Publishing Group for giving me permission to quote extensively from Sir Ian's autobiography, *Blood, Sweat and Cheers* and from a passage in the *BMJ* 1995, I:727. I would like to thank Carol Graham for permission to use her striking and lifelike portrait of Sir Ian with his dog Rory. Thanks are also due to *The Belfast Telegraph*, Bobby Studio Dublin, Diplomat Photography Washington DC, Christopher Hill Belfast, Wilfred Green Belfast and Robin Humphreys for permission to reproduce the photographs.

RICHARD CLARKE

Chapter 1

Antecedents

SCOTTISH ROOTS – JAMES FRASER

The Fraser family can be traced back to James Fraser, crofter, and Mary Cuming. Their son John Fraser, crofter, of Bunoich, Fort Augustus, near Inverness (19 April 1803 – 7 July 1875) married Margaret Tulloch (4 April 1796 – 13 March 1875). Their son James Fraser was born on 13 January 1831 and when he was a young man acted as tutor to the Ellice family of Invergarry Castle, about six miles south-west of Fort Augustus. They gave him a copy of Boswell's *Life of Johnson* as a parting gift before he went on to teach at Glenquoich School nearby. It was therefore to Mrs Ellice that he turned in January 1854 for a recommendation to obtain a post in the Department of Customs and Excise. He kept a copy of the very flowery letter to her asking for her help, as follows:

> Madam, I humbly beg to take the liberty of soliciting your influence with Mr Wood, Chairman of the Board of Excise, in order to admit me into his service in the capacity of an Inland Revenue Officer. I am now twenty-three years of age and I feel very anxious to be employed in that department of H M Service. If you deem me qualified to discharge the duties of such an office, I humbly trust that you will be kind enough to recommend me to the favourable consideration of the Chairman with the view to confer on me this lasting favour. And if you will be kind enough to favour me in this matter I shall hope that a grateful remembrance of your kindness shall never be effaced from my mind amid all the hardships which I may have to encounter in performing my duties, that it will prove to me a stimulus to exertion that you had so kindly interested yourself in my behalf. I have honour to be, madam, your obedt. and humble servant. James Fraser.

James was appointed an 'expectant' or 'proper officer' in February 1854. A notebook of this period gives tables relating to excise duty payable on whisky distilled. More usefully to us, it gives details of his career and of the dates of birth and death of his immediate family. In his first year he was posted for a few weeks at a time to Inverness, Fortwilliam, Nairn, Fort Augustus, Alness and Brechin. In 1855–6 he covered Dundee, Brechin, Montrose and Cupar before becoming an 'assistant' in May 1856. Thereafter he seems to have travelled less but covered Lanholm, Falkirk and Paisley, before being promoted to 'ride officer' in Londonderry in August 1857.

By 1859, being now 28, James could really think of settling down. On 8 September 1859 he married, in Carndonagh Presbyterian Church, Catherine Ann Moore, eldest daughter of Robert Moore of Churchtown, Carndonagh (about twenty miles north of Londonderry) and Jane Wilson. Robert and his brother Alexander shared a farm of over 100 acres, and it is said that during the famine of 1846–7 Robert earned himself the title of 'the Poor Man's Friend'.

By the time of the marriage James seems to have been accepted readily into his new community, for he received a book 'from a few of his friends in Carndonagh congregation' as 'a token of esteem and an acknowledgement of his efforts to improve the young in sacred music. AD 1859'.

A reminder of the transport problems of an excise officer in those days is given by his accounts for keeping a horse during the year 1862.

Date	Product/Service	£	s	d
Jan 11	5 stooks of straw		2	6
13	12 stone oats		10	0
18	half set shoes		1	0
24	30 stone oats	1	7	6
Feb 10	13 stone oats		11	3
April 7	15 stone oats		12	6
28	8 stone oats		7	4
28	Straw		5	0
May 26	21 stone oats		19	3
26	horse shoeing		2	0
June 26	horse shoeing		1	6
Aug 20	17 stone oats	1	0	6
29	horse shoeing		2	0
29	repairing of car		1	10
Sept 9	1 ton hay	2	10	0
12	1 ton hay	3	0	0
Oct 13	8 stone oats		7	0
Nov 1	horse shoeing		2	0
12	2 stone oats		2	0
17	19 stone oats		14	3
20	1 cwt bran and carriage		6	8

It is not, of course, clear whether he kept more than one horse, but the reference to 'repairing of car' indicates that as well as travelling on horseback he may have sometimes travelled by horse-drawn car. Expenses would also have included wages for a groom to look after the horse.

In 1859 Catherine was 38, ten years older than James, but they had a long and happy marriage and three children. The first of them, Jane (Jeannie) (9 November 1860 – 6 September 1933), and the next, John James (30 September 1862 – 25 May 1880), were born in Ireland, but in September 1864, before the arrival of the third, James was posted back to Scotland, first to Pitlochry and then to Crieff. Robert Moore Fraser was born at Crieff on 10 February 1865. Meanwhile James Fraser continued to move up the promotion ladder, as examiner in 1868 and supervisor at Ballater in 1869. He was moved briefly to Logan in 1873 and his final move was back to Ireland as supervisor of the Belfast Office, in October 1873.

James and his family had a succession of houses in various parts of Belfast: 81 Springfield Terrace around 1875, 10 Cameron Street from *c.*1876 to 1890, and then in Plevna Street. He retired in 1896 at the age of 65 and moved in 1902 across Belfast to the newly-built 33 Cyprus Gardens, Knock, where he died on 4 January 1908. His widow followed on 22 December 1909; both were buried in Antrim New Cemetery. Robert had recently bought the grave plot at Antrim when his first wife died, so his parents and sister were buried there too.

James Fraser's three children grew up in the various family homes, but the elder son 'ran away to sea' and died of fever at sea on 25 May 1880 at the age of 17. We know little of the family life at home except that James was strict in matters of religion and domestic life, and perhaps that is why John James left. However, we have a wonderfully detailed account of a Moore family wedding a little later, which emphasizes the continued links with Donegal and shows that life in the Moore circle at least could he great fun.

The family farm at Churchtown had passed from Alexander to Catherine's younger brother Robert and in 1889 the family celebrated the wedding of his daughter Mary Jane (Minnie) to the Rev. Robert Morrison, minister of Carndonagh. It was the occasion for a great gathering of family and friends, so Jane and Robert Moore Fraser made their way by train to a station opposite Culmore Point, crossed in the ferry and were met by a horse-drawn 'car' for the three-hour journey to Carndonagh. They stayed at Churchtown and on the following morning helped to prepare the wedding breakfast. The wedding ceremony at noon proceeded according to plan, followed by the wedding breakfast and speeches at two o'clock. The bride and groom then left and the guests regrouped for an evening of dancing. They sprinkled the floor of the hay-loft with water, polished it with shavings of candle wax and made up an impromptu entertainment. This consisted of a fiddler and volunteer singers and reciters, with supper at 2.00 a.m. Finally, Robert stayed at the manse where the men slept two in a bed, and Jeannie stayed at Churchtown. On the next day Robert Moore took the ladies for a drive to Carrickabrahy Castle on Doagh Island. Unfortunately it started to rain heavily and he miscalculated the tides, so by the evening the ladies were 'soaked like a wet sponge'. The remaining members of the party seem to have spent the day cutting up pieces of 'bridescake' and parcelling them for dispatch, as well as preparing an account of the wedding to go into the *Derry Standard*. Jane and Robert had a total of a fortnight in the area, visiting local families and going for picnics and to church on Sunday, before they returned home to Belfast.

James Fraser's will (of 14 April 1899) provides for the family in the approved manner of the time. His gold watch, chain and locket and, interestingly, his 'library of books' were to go to Robert. Other belongings and money were to pass to his widow for life and then to his son, but with an annuity of £52 for Jane. It is clear that the family home, as was the custom a hundred years ago, was rented. This facilitated much greater mobility than at present and of course predated the era when house property prices rose in such a dramatic way. The £52 annuity also dates from a time when it represented an adequate subsistence, and inflation did not continually eat into it. Jane Fraser moved later to Bryansford, where she died unmarried on 6 September 1933.

DR ROBERT MOORE FRASER

Robert Moore Fraser, having been born in Crieff on 10 February 1865, was educated first at Ballater Female School, where he won a prize in March 1871. He came with the family to Belfast in 1873 and went to school at the Royal Belfast Academical Institution ('Inst') in 1877. His brother John James had been there from 1875. Robert won at least two prizes from Inst in 1877 and 1878. At school he was thinking of joining the Indian Civil Service, and in keeping with this he developed a clear style of handwriting. He also considered going to China as a missionary with the China Inland Mission, but abandoned this idea when John James died (1880) and he felt he must stay at home to look after his elderly parents.

Robert went on to Queen's College, as Queen's University was then known, matriculating in 1882 and taking the BA degree in 1885. This may have been to keep his options open for a career, but many medical students at Queen's did so at that time as well as all those at Trinity College Dublin. He preserved his knowledge of Latin and Greek until late in life and his son remembered him then reading his Greek testament.

He studied medicine in the years 1885–90 at Queen's College and the Belfast Royal Hospital under the various distinguished physicians and surgeons of the day. These included Professor James

Cuming, the intellectual and cautious professor of medicine, and Dr William Whitla (later Professor Sir William Whitla), prolific writer of textbooks and benefactor of Belfast and its university. On the surgical side he would have been taught by Professor Thomas Sinclair, young, dapper and newly appointed, and Mr Henry O'Neill. The latter's main claim to fame was a lineal descent from Hugh O'Neill of Tyrone, the great Irish leader in Elizabethan times. He was also founder and first president of the Belfast Medical Students' Association, a leading advocate of public health for the city, and eventually became Lord Mayor. He signed and gave Robert Fraser a present of a book, *Landmarks Medical and Surgical* by Luther Holden, dated 1 February 1890 – a time when Robert would have been working for his final examination.

Robert took the medical degrees of MB BCh BAO (the standard then as now) in 1890. Before 1908 students of Queen's College, Belfast were examined by the Royal University of Ireland as well as those of other Irish colleges. Examinations were therefore taken, and degrees given, in Dublin. He immediately started into general practice at 211 Albertbridge Road, Belfast and remained there essentially for the rest of his working life.

He lived the life of a busy single-handed GP, on call all the time, paid erratically and often in kind rather than in cash, risking his own life with every 'fever' patient he visited, but with a level of job satisfaction rarely seen in the UK today. He also had one luxury in his busy life that his father did not have – a motor car. His first car was a five horsepower Vauxhall bought in the early years of the century from the Chambers brothers, who were the first car engineers and dealers of the city. It was, of course, always breaking down or getting punctures and over the years the horse or bicycle was always needed in reserve. Indeed, he always loved the bicycle and rode it for pleasure almost to the end of his life.

One of the classic problems with driving a car at that time was in starting it with a crank handle. This was surprisingly effective most of the time, and one twist was usually sufficient. However, if the engine backfired the handle whipped backwards, causing a 'chauffeur's fracture'. On one occasion in the 1920s this happened to Robert, and one of his most distinguished contemporaries, Robert Campbell FRCS, was sent for. He appeared in a few minutes and set the fracture in the drawing room, which happened to be filled with hand painted table-mats being prepared by Mrs Fraser for the local church bazaar. In fact, Robert Campbell, having been roughly contemporary with Robert Fraser, was often called out for surgical consultations by the latter and Ian got to know him as a family friend as well as a teacher.

There was, of course, no such thing as postgraduate education, nor were there any refresher courses, but contact with hospital medicine was maintained even more than at present. For instance, Robert attended the UVF hospital (then at the back of Queen's) once or twice a week during the First World War to give anaesthetics. In addition the general practitioner would call out an attending physician or surgeon to give a second opinion or perhaps to operate. During an operation the GP might be asked to give the anaesthetic. Such calls were essential for the hospital doctor's livelihood, but they had a reciprocal benefit in keeping the GP up to date.

MARRIAGE AND FAMILY

While still a medical student Robert met his future wife, Margaret Boal Ferguson, second daughter of Adam Boal Ferguson (who is described on the marriage certificate as a mill manager, of Carrickfergus) and Mary Ann Molyneux. The Ferguson family home was at Larkhill, Muckamore, where they had a good farm. Robert and Margaret were married in Fortwilliam Presbyterian Church, Belfast, on 1 February 1900. She was then aged 31 and developed pulmonary tuberculosis when pregnant with their son Ian, who was born on 9 February 1901 at 211 Albertbridge Road. Ian was, in fact, registered as John James Fraser, called after his uncle who died at sea, but he seems to have been known as Ian James at least from the time he went to school, and later as simply Ian.

There was no effective treatment for tuberculosis at that time, and Margaret died on 10 November 1903. She was buried in Antrim New Cemetery near the Ferguson family grave. Robert must have had a terrible few years at this stage, with his wife's terminal illness and a new baby to look after. Following her death he adopted the only possible solution and asked his ageing parents to look after Ian. They were very kind and not too far away in Cyprus Gardens, but Ian describes it as a strict puritan household in the Scottish presbyterian tradition, with the blinds drawn and all forms of pleasure forbidden on Sunday.

Robert Fraser married secondly in Dundela (Knock) Presbyterian Church, on 11 June 1907, Alice Josephine Cuthbert, youngest child of Dr Alexander Cuthbert of Londonderry. One of the witnesses (what would now be called the 'best man') was Harry P. Swan. He was a notable folklorist and local historian from Buncrana, as well as being a successful businessman in flour milling. He was author of many books on the area of Inishowen and had a collection of small antiquities from the area, many of which are now in the National Museum of Ireland.

Dr Cuthbert's family lived in and around Londonderry for several generations and he had graduated MD in 1856 after studying at Queen's College, Belfast. He was a successful general practitioner in the Waterside, becoming in 1874 superintendent medical officer of health for Londonderry. One of his most interesting achievements was to write a paper (1863) with Dr Thomas H. Babington on 'Caisson disease', then an almost unknown condition, in workmen who had worked under pressure in the building of the new Foyle bridge. The period of exposure to high barometric pressure in the 'caisson' resulted in progressive build-up of nitrogen in the central nervous system. Too rapid decompression then released these gases as bubbles in the tissues, causing 'the bends' and even paralysis or death. Sadly, Alexander Cuthbert died (along with a district nurse), on 1 March 1876, of typhus fever contracted while visiting a sick patient.

Robert's marriage naturally led to young Ian's return to his father's home, and, as he says in his memoir, 'No one was brought up in a happier home, and I cannot be grateful enough' (Fraser, 1989, p. 5). In fact he regarded Alice so completely as his mother that he refers to her frequently as such and even to her father, Dr Cuthbert, as his grandfather. Dr Fraser's second marriage was long and happy and they had one child, Margaret (Peggy) Cuthbert Fraser, who was born on 18 May 1911. She never married but lived at home, and looked after her parents in their old age.

Robert had moved to 223 Albertbridge Road and continued to practise there until his retirement around 1930. In 1920, rather unusually for a busy and senior general practitioner, Robert prepared a thesis for the degree of MD, which was duly awarded. The thesis was entitled 'Albuminuria: its significance in apparently healthy male lives'. It is based on the urine analysis and follow-up of a group of individuals seen over an 18-year period for life insurance examination: as Robert says, the general practitioner is better placed than the hospital doctor for this sort of study.

The family moved out to Gortfoyle, 364 Upper Newtownards Road (called after Dr Cuthbert's house in Londonderry), after his second marriage and moved in 1939 to 10 Winston Gardens, just 100 yards away. There he died on 28 January 1952, followed by Alice on 14 August 1953. They were buried in Dundonald City Cemetery. Margaret Fraser never had a career, and after her parents died she moved to a bungalow at 20 Clover Hill Park.

Chapter 2

School and university

CHILDHOOD

Ian Fraser grew up at Gortfoyle with his father and stepmother and his early family letters indicate the usual interests of boys – stamp collecting, a family dog, and holidays with his Moore relations at Churchtown, Carndonagh. His aunt Sarah Ferguson wrote to him from Larkhill in 1913 telling him of the progress of the various flowers in the garden and the crops and livestock on the farm. It is evident that he knew it well and that there was a strong bond with his Ferguson grandparents as well as with his aunts Ellen and Sarah who were also living there. At home his father was a strict disciplinarian, but religious observance was not as severe as with his grandfather, and all was softened by his stepmother's care and affection. Family holidays throughout Ian's childhood were usually spent on the Irish coast – Ballycastle, Rossnowlagh or Portstewart – broken only by an unfortunately timed holiday in Boulogne in 1914.

His first schools were Miss Corry and Miss Brown's School in North Road in 1907 and Miss Wylie's Dame School at Knock Road, with a year at home before he obtained a three-year scholarship in 1913 to his father's old school, 'Inst' – an easy tram ride from home. His stepmother would have preferred the convenience of Campbell College, but Robert was an exact contemporary of R.M. Jones, probably Inst's most distinguished headmaster ever (Jamieson, 1959), and was clearly impressed by its advantages.

R.M. Jones had come to Inst in 1898 and set about transforming the school and broadening its educational possibilities. This required money, and he took the controversial step of giving a long lease of the ground to the north-east of the school to the Belfast Technical College (1900); while one regrets the resulting disfigurement of the distinguished Inst facade, the annual rent to Inst was the then enormous sum of £1,350. Other sites along College Square North, including that of the Whitla Medical Institute, added to this income. Jones also closed the old boarding accommodation, in the top floor, and his own living accommodation when he moved off the school premises. In their place new physics and chemistry laboratories and a Commercial Department were created, plus a Common Hall in the centre of the first floor. Of special interest in relation to the Royal Victoria Hospital, which was being built at the same time, a new boiler house and plenum system of ventilation were introduced in 1901, described then as providing 'a constant supply of air that was warm and pure'. Other administrative changes included a better fee structure, many new departmental head teachers and higher pay for all the staff. When young Ian went to Inst in 1913, it had just celebrated the centenary of its Charter and had truly moved into the twentieth century.

Ian remained at Inst for five years, with a strong and balanced school career. He won many school prizes and honours in all the Intermediate Board Exams, but also enjoyed acting in the school plays. The highlight of his acting career was as Monsieur Jourdain in Molière's *Le Bourgeois Gentilhomme*, where he 'acted to a nicety the pompous blustering stupidity of the upstart aspirant to nobility, with his fine raiment, his aristocratic airs and his blind worship of "les gens de qualité"'. He portrayed well 'the blank astonishment of Monsieur Jourdain when he discovers he has been talking prose for the last half century without knowing it' (*School News*). His near contemporary Dr H.G. Calwell was also in this production. Rugby had developed considerably since the introduction of the Medallion Shield competition in 1910, and although he was not heavy enough for the First XV, he did play in the under-15 team.

However, the dominant influence on school life was the First World War, and later he was to recall the solemn ceremony of reading out at the Friday Assembly Meeting the names of the old boys who had been killed. These were often boys who had distinguished themselves at rugby or elsewhere, and it made a strong impression on Ian. Inst had formed an Officers' Training Corps early in the war, and one of Ian's memories was of 'trench warfare' in the field at the back of the school. In the course of this they threw dummy hand grenades (obtained from Mackie's foundry nearby) across no man's land into the enemy lines. Before throwing the grenade the pin was pulled out and the thrower counted '101, 102, 103, 104' and threw. The grenade exploded at '105', and the trick was not to throw it too soon in case the recipients had time to return it before it exploded. On the other hand, the grenade was heavy and it took practice and some strength to get it out of one's own lines and into those of the enemy. Clearly the experience was sufficiently close to the real thing to appeal to the boys.

They learned to wear uniform, in particular the now outmoded puttees which cut off the circulation if they were too tight and fell off if they were too loose. They also learned to send messages by semaphore and Morse, though by the time Ian had any possibility of using them, in the Second World War, loudhailer and radio had replaced them. Instead of a summer camp they went off to County Londonderry to pull flax. Linen was important for aeroplane wings and the supplies from Belgium and Russia had dried up, so it suddenly became worth while to grow the crop in Ulster (as it did again in the Second World War).

Choosing a career was not difficult for Ian; like so many doctors' sons, he decided to study medicine at Queen's. In this choice he was influenced not only by his father's life but by tales of his stepmother's father in Londonderry who had died of typhus looking after his patients. Yet another influence then and later in his career was the example of an old Instonian, Captain (later Brigadier) Sinton of the Indian Medical Service, who was unique in being an FRS as well as being awarded the VC for gallantry in action and disregard for his own safety in caring for the wounded. Finally, there was Professor Almroth Wright who had left Inst to follow a distinguished career in bacteriology at St Mary's, London and was a founder of the new science of immunology.

UNIVERSITY

Ian started his medical studies at Queen's in September 1918. He commented later that he did not enjoy his early years as a student but when he reached the clinical stage in the Royal Victoria Hospital, his enthusiasm was really kindled. Even if he did not enjoy the work at least he kept at it, unlike a neighbour at one of the botany lectures who was heard to mutter 'I'm not interested in this xylem and phloem stuff – I want to know when the pubs open'. Inevitably the neighbour left the course, to run a business selling refrigerators, and very successfully too. Probably botany remained the most boring and irrelevant part of the medical course until it was absorbed into biology, and later the first year was dropped altogether.

1918 was a year when many servicemen were given early release from the army and a grant to study medicine. They formed nearly fifty per cent of the year and, as they usually were highly motivated, provided strong competition throughout the course. The overall numbers were also large, and even with some 'dropouts' 120 students graduated, 13 of them with honours. This meant that in the anatomy department, with a shortage of bodies, there would be at least 28 people round each cadaver.

Professor Johnson Symington had a stroke while Ian was a student, and did not return to work. The vacancy was temporarily filled by P.T. Crymble and Margaret Purce, sister of the surgeon Barney Purce. She had already taken the FRCS and was to become a brilliant ear, nose and throat surgeon in England. Symington's successor, Professor Thomas Walmsley, did not take over until 1919 – after Ian had moved on – but was in post by the time Ian returned as anatomy demonstrator in 1924.

In the 1920s the great majority of students from Belfast went to the Rotunda Hospital in Dublin to gain their midwifery experience. However, Ian decided to stay in Belfast and go to the Ulster Hospital for Women and Children in Templemore Avenue, which was just down the road from his home in Knock. He knew it well, as he had just taken his children's diseases certificate there also. The requirement for the midwifery certificate was to deliver twenty babies 'on the District', i.e. in the patient's own home. The call for a delivery would come from the hospital in the middle of the night only to be taken by Ian's father, who was delighted to find that it was for Ian and not himself. Ian was duly woken up, dressed, got out his bicycle, lit his oil lamp and cycled down to the hospital to collect a card with the address of the lady in labour. He then would have to find one of the streets off the Newtownards Road, which then (as now) were sharply divided into Nationalist and Unionist. On one occasion he was stopped late at night by an officious young vigilante who told him to go away. Ian duly turned round, saying that he was very glad to do so and get back to bed. At this the young man followed him and after some delay Ian told him that he had come to a maternity case but that the man's interference meant that it was probably now too late and the baby might even have died. This produced an immediate reaction and Ian was rushed to the house for red-carpet treatment. In fact, he had to wait another two or three hours before the baby was born. Ian also recalls that during his studies of midwifery he told the sister in the operating theatre of the old Maternity Hospital in Townsend Street that he had never seen a caesarean section. She phoned up two days later to say that Mr Tommy Holmes was doing one that afternoon. This was in 1921, when rioting was frequent, and Ian had to lie on the floor of the tram and creep along close to the wall in Townsend Street while bullets ricocheted off the road.

CLINICAL TEACHERS

In hospital the chair of medicine had moved on from the therapeutic nihilist James Cuming of Robert Fraser's day to the pedantic James Lindsay, who was probably equally uninspiring to the medical student. A cardiac murmur had to be described as 'rough, rumbling and ingravescent', otherwise the student was wrong – incidentally, the same phraseology was still in use 50 years later. When Professor Lindsay retired in 1923 he was succeeded in the chair by W.W.D. Thomson, who probably contributed far more to Ian's knowledge of medicine. 'W.W.D.' had obtained first class honours in his MB and gold medal in his MD as well as having served in the war. He was the last of the old-style professors who made their mark not by research but by bedside teaching. He had a County Down drawl and a wise and relaxed approach to doctors and patients. As a result his opinion was sought as often by general practitioners in the country villages as by colleagues in University Square.

Two of the older professors, Sir William Whitla and Sir John Byers, retired about the time Ian joined Queen's as a student, but

Professor Thomas Sinclair was still in post after 32 years. Ian describes him as follows:

> He often wore spats and always a white lining to his waistcoat and as he talked at the bedside he kept the fob of his watch chain spinning round all the time. Before an operation he always sat down with his eyes closed for a short time. We never knew whether he was saying a quick prayer or revising his anatomy, or perhaps just having a short snooze. Once into action, however, he did a magnificent job. (Fraser, *Blood, Sweat and Cheers*, 1989, p. 19; all extracts from this publication are reproduced by permission of the BMJ Publishing Group)

Ian's views of teaching (and of academics) are well shown in the following passage:

> I always think that undergraduate teaching is best performed by the general surgeon who is in the day-to-day hurly-burly of a busy practice. It is only a man of that sort who can tell students what to do on a domiciliary visit. He can explain the difficulty of doing a rectal examination on a fat patient in the depth of a feather bed, and he can explain the acrobatics necessary to avoid being engulfed in the depth of this bed together with the patient. No full time professor of surgery ever had that exciting experience. For him the patient is sitting ready for the examination, teed up like a golf ball on the first tee. (Fraser, 1989, p. 24)

The general surgeons of the post-war period included Mr Arthur Brownlow Mitchell, (Mr) Thomas Sinclair Kirk and Mr (later Professor) Andrew Fullerton. Ian Fraser has characterized them all. A.B. Mitchell was clearly a sound and straightforward surgeon and was one of the founders of the Association of Surgeons and the first surgical gastroenterologist in Belfast, with a personal series of 16 perforated duodenal ulcers without a death. The next generation of Ian's surgical teachers, who served in the war and were appointed to the RVH staff just afterwards, were S.T. Irwin and R.J. McConnell. Irwin was a broadly based general surgeon but had a special interest in orthopaedics and peptic ulcer surgery. McConnell remained a general surgeon and a particularly popular teacher. Later Ian assisted him frequently during his domiciliary surgery and says 'Later when I myself did a lot of domiciliary operations I always felt that I owed everything that I did to my training with R.J. McConnell' (Fraser, 1993).

Thomas Sinclair Kirk, for many years senior surgeon in the Royal Victoria Hospital, can hardly be defined as a teacher and Ian treats him with ridicule throughout his writings. Kirk's main problem was that he always believed that he was right in spite of common sense or other people's views. He sat once for his FRCS and was failed, wrongfully as he thought, so he refused to try again. Thereafter he was known as 'Surgeon Kirk' but not 'Mr Kirk'. He made all his patients with abdominal drains lie on their face because, as he said, 'fluid naturally goes downhill rather than uphill'. (However, the nursing staff made this more tolerable by restricting it to times when he would visit the ward.) Large wounds, such as the raw area after removal of a breast, he filled with several tablespoonfuls of urea crystals. The crystals were very deliquescent and ensured that the wounds discharged freely for several days. This story is embellished by the report of a patient who came back to the surgeon six months after a mastectomy with some 10–12 nodules present in the scar – thought at first to be recurrences of the original cancer, though on biopsy they contained nothing more than broken glass. It turned out that an over-conscientious ward sister, of a saving temperament, had swept all the urea from an old broken container into a new one when the original had broken into small pieces.

The stories of Surgeon Kirk are legion and remained with Ian all his life. Throughout his eighties Ian would propose the health of the staff at the annual medical staff dinner and pass round Kirk's 'loving cup'. Ian would recount how the cup had been presented to Kirk by the staff on his retirement and returned by Kirk's family when he died. However, he usually added that Kirk was one of the most unloving men he had known.

In complete contrast is Ian's portrayal of his mentor Andrew Fullerton, who had just returned from the war when Ian first attended the Royal Victoria but was not appointed to the chair of surgery until 1923 (Chapter 3). The other surgical specialities are also well portrayed. The new professor of gynaecology, R.J. Johnstone, 'operated rapidly and skilfully with less instruments than I have ever seen anyone use before or since, perhaps three or four artery forceps. On one occasion some Americans came into the theatre and they were heard to say "Professor you sure go light on the hardware"'(Fraser, 1989). Johnstone was apparently not very interested in teaching, and adopted the convenient philosophy that a 40 minute lecture was all that a student's brain or gluteus maximus could stand. This, of course also suited Ian and the students generally, but they clearly preferred the professor of midwifery, C.G. Lowry, who was slower in both operating and lecturing. His more didactic method of teaching gave them excellent notes for future use.

C.G. Lowry was the moving force behind the new Royal Maternity Hospital, added beside the Royal Victoria Hospital in 1933. This not only benefited the patients but also meant that there was no need for any students to go to the Rotunda, though it must be said that they went to Dublin as much for the social life as for the obstetric experience.

WORK AND LEISURE

Ian's academic prowess at university and Royal Victoria Hospital can be judged by the succession of prizes he obtained – physics, chemistry, zoology, botany, anatomy (1919), anatomy prize and special exhibition (1920), pharmacy (1921), medicine, gynaecology and midwifery (1922), Malcolm exhibition (jointly) (1921), Coulter exhibition (runner-up) 1922, McQuitty scholarship (1923), and first class honours and first place in each subject in the final MB BCh BAO examination (1923), giving him two further exhibitions. He was also awarded the Gold Medal of the Ulster Hospital for Women and Children. All these achievements are summarized in Mr S.T. Irwin's testimonial that 'he showed an ability and industry rarely found in the medical student'.

Professor W.W.D. Thomson commented in his testimonial for Ian: 'Often a brilliant student is so absorbed in his work as to take little interest in the life of the university; but Mr Fraser always took a leading part in the social aspects of his university training, and was again and again elected to fill offices of responsibility and trust.' We know that he was actively involved in rugby, hockey and golf; he gave up the rugby at university because his small build left him at the mercy of the heavyweights who dominated the game, but he kept up hockey for many years.

An example of Ian's social life at the university can be gleaned from his description of the Queen's Officers' Training Corps (OTC).

The war was now over, and it had a much more relaxed atmosphere than the OTC at Inst. Indeed it sounds like one long party! The most active part was the medical section, which was prominent in the band and the Pierrot company known as the Queen's Jesters. Notable among these were the future Dr Sydney Allison, neurologist, and Air-Vice Marshal Sir William Tyrrell, but the person who most skilfully combined medicine and the stage was Dr Richard (Dicky) Hunter. He was at that time the lecturer in the Anatomy department but had an artistic career ranging from being a member of the 'Claque' in Paris to ringmaster in the Belfast Circus. The annual camp of the Territorial Army occasionally got 'out of hand', and after one notorious visit to the Isle of Man, they were asked never to return. They were also banned from Warrenpoint.

It must be remembered that Ian was basically living at home while at university, and this must have exerted some restraining influence. Family holidays were still usually taken in Ballycastle or Donegal, but he did get away to France in the summer of 1921. This trip was essentially a four-week course in Paris with lectures and ward rounds in the main hospitals. (Ian was throughout his life a good French speaker.) He and a cousin, Sandy McConnell, had planned to follow this by a touring holiday around France in Sandy's motorcycle with sidecar. However, when Sandy arrived in Paris it was clear that this would not be possible as the machine was not reliable enough. Ian managed to see quite a lot of Paris and its surroundings between parts of the course, which indeed was not really up to expectations in intensity of teaching or quality generally. Then they set off on a circuitous journey to Dieppe, visiting all the smaller towns on the way. As usual with students, much of the correspondence home is taken up with descriptions of the food and their efforts to economize. What is really striking is how much trouble the motorcycle gave, between punctures, belt slipping in the rain, etc., etc.; also the poor quality of their protective clothing compared with that of the present day. As a result they never managed more than 100 miles in a day, even on the straight run north through England. In the end they managed to get home safely but penniless, in time for a free family holiday in Clovelly in Devonshire.

Ian's time at university culminated in his graduating with first-class honours, and a wide field was open to him. He wanted to hold a house physician/surgeon post in the Royal Victoria Hospital but it had been decided that the 13 posts should go to ex-servicemen who had obtained honours, and there were 13 of these. In the end one dropped out because he needed to get into general practice at once, leaving Ian with the coveted post.

Chapter 3

Surgical training and early years

RESIDENT MEDICAL OFFICER

Dr Ian Fraser, as we have seen, became a resident house surgeon and house physician and extern surgeon at the Royal Victoria Hospital in 1923. The jump from medical student with the single goal of passing final MB (as well as possible) to resident doctor with responsibility for many patients is a severe shock, but the stress was much greater when there were far fewer intermediaries in the ward. He has left us a general picture of the innovations about this time (which imposed an additional worry); the first of these was blood transfusion. Landsteiner had identified blood groups in 1900 and some progress in transfusion had come during the First World War, often using direct donor artery to patient vein transfusion. The alternative was storing blood that had been anticoagulated with citrate or defibrination. The technique was used intermittently throughout the 1920s and 1930s but there was little real progress until the Spanish Civil War and the Second World War.

One of the more bizarre duties of the house physician was in the treatment of GPI (general paralysis of the insane or tertiary syphilis). Someone had observed on a troopship bringing back soldiers from the Far East that some who acquired malaria had a dramatic improvement in their neurological symptoms. So, when a patient with GPI came into the ward the senior physician asked Ian to take the patient in his motorcycle and sidecar, to another hospital where there was a known case of malaria. The patient was given 10 ml of malarial blood, and inevitably developed a high temperature. A few days later he died, giving 100 per cent mortality in the highly uncontrolled trial.

Another tale of his motorcycle in this period describes how he was rushing away from the hospital on a Saturday afternoon to play hockey. Suddenly a little girl of about 10 dashed into the road and Ian had the misfortune to knock her down. A crowd soon gathered and, although the girl got up and ran off, one of the bystanders chipped in with 'I saw you coming down like the hammers of Hell'. A crowd was gathering and things were beginning to look bad for Ian when an enormous man pushed forward with 'I never saw better driving; many men would have killed that girl.' At this point the crowd began to melt away and when Ian turned to thank his unexpected advocate, it transpired that the latter had not seen the accident at all but had been in the pub. However, he had recognized Ian as the young doctor looking after his 'missus' in the hospital and giving her 'bloody good treatment'. Ian then assured him that if she had had good treatment to date it was nothing to what she was going to get from now on!

The resident doctor of those days had a much more varied life than more recently and in fact carried out many tasks in the field of clinical chemistry. These ranged from testing urine for sugar by boiling with Fehling's solution (with the risk of it spurting over oneself or a colleague) to the prolonged labour of assessing gastric acidity in an ulcer patient with a fractional test meal. This was an unpleasant business requiring the passage of a Ryle's tube into the patient's stomach, feeding him a gruel and taking samples of gastric juice half hourly. However, the resultant graph of gastric acid secretion did give an indication of the possible value of surgery.

Yet another tale of the house surgeon's duties, this time in the gynaecological wards, is of going down to the Liverpool–Belfast boat in the early morning to collect a tube of radon for insertion into the uterus. Ian had first to find out exactly when the boat was expected to dock and to phone the surgeon to enable him to have the patient on the operating table and anaesthetized. It was later realized that the whole procedure was largely a waste of time, as the radon would have lost 50 per cent of its radioactivity over the 24 hours taken to travel from central London to the Belfast nursing home.

TRAINING AS A SURGEON

The year spent as house physician and surgeon convinced Ian that he wanted to be a surgeon, and he spent the following academic year, 1924–5, as demonstrator in anatomy at Queen's University. While in the department he strengthened his friendship with Dicky Hunter, who had been appointed lecturer in 1924, and we may be sure that it was like returning to the old outrageous student days. In spite of this he started working for the first part of his Irish primary fellowship in surgery, and consolidated this in the autumn by attending a course on anatomy and physiology at the Middlesex Hospital, London. It was his first real stay away from home, and London can be a fairly bleak place on one's own with no income and pressure to work all the time. He had a few friends from Belfast working in London (Drs Samuel S. Brown, R. Leslie Dodds and H. Hilton Stewart), but seems to have restricted social contacts rigorously to a few meals out and visits to various churches. Fortunately he passed both the Dublin and London primary fellowship examinations in December 1925, gaining first place in each subject in Dublin. Once the exams were over, he was able to return home for Christmas and a well-earned rest. He later obtained a testimonial from Professor Thomas Yeates, Professor of Anatomy at the Middlesex Hospital, which along with other complimentary remarks, describes him as 'the most brilliant student in a class for the primary fellowship consisting of some of the best students from all parts of the world'.

After this year he was at a loose end, having applied unsuccessfully for over 20 house surgeon posts in England. Then in early 1926 he was invited to stand in for the Resident Surgical Officer in St Helens, Lancashire, who had to resign suddenly. This was his first experience of hospital medicine outside Ireland, and the excitement was unexpectedly increased by his finding a general strike when he disembarked from the Belfast–Liverpool ferry. At 7.00 a.m. there was no transport of any sort, and he was faced with a journey of 20 miles with a heavy bag. The position seemed hopeless until he discovered a small greengrocer's cart loaded to the top with bags of potatoes, carrots, sprouts, etc., with a pony between the shafts and a rather unshaven gentleman in charge. What really mattered was that there was a small plate on one of the shafts that said 'John Gribbon, greengrocer, St Helens'. Ian approached him and with great deference suggested that for £2 perhaps he might sit on one of the bags of potatoes as far as the hospital at St Helen's. After a small monetary adjustment to £3, he mounted the cart and eventually made his state entry to his new job mounted on a bag of spuds!

While the strike was going on, Ian decided to attend one of the strike meetings along with about 1,000 miners. Naturally he put on an old dusty suit to try to look inconspicuous, but he didn't reckon on the miners' ability to hunker down to listen to the speaker. Fifteen minutes was more than enough for him and he had to stand up, making him the only visible figure in a vast crowd. In the end he was lucky to get away with a few curses in English and Welsh.

Ian's letters home indicate that the stay in St Helens was hard work with plenty of responsibility and plenty of clinical experience. The hospital was a typical small voluntary hospital with the usual range of specialities of the period, and Ian carried out hysterectomies, general abdominal surgery and mastoids, managed poisonings and gave blood transfusions. He comments pretty acidly about the local understanding of blood transfusion and found he had to enrol and group donors, take the blood and finally administer it. (Having done all this as a house surgeon at home, he probably thought there should be someone junior to do it in St Helens!) Apart from learning by experience there were experts in Liverpool such as Blair Bell (gynaecology) and Ian McMurray (orthopaedics) who were only too happy to help young doctors.

He did have some leisure, however, and although there are references to dances missed and invitations turned down, he clearly had a busy social life, asking in letters for his golf clubs and 'suit of tails'. One of the most entertaining of the dinners was a reunion of Queen's medical graduates in Liverpool. This included no fewer than 37 doctors: one Thomas Clarke had entered Queen's in 1863 and a more recent graduate, Dr Augustus ('Gusy') Merrick, was a GP on the staff of St Helens. As Ian says, it was funny to hear the older folk talking of Professors Gordon, Seaton Reid and Cuming as if they were personal friends.

The light operas of Gilbert and Sullivan were a life-long interest of Ian's, and he managed to see the D'Oyly Carte performing *Iolanthe* and *The Gondoliers* in Liverpool. A more ambitious weekend trip was to London for a show and a visit to Twickenham, but such weekends off were always uncertain.

Ian's big adventure while at St Helens was after a pit disaster near by, and though his account in a letter home is brief it doesn't need much imagination to picture the scene. Two men had been trapped by a roof fall, and it was feared that amputation of a limb might be necessary. A call came to the hospital and Ian volunteered to go down along with Dr Campbell, the pit medical officer. They descended 600 yards in a lift and then had to walk 1,400 yards to reach the coalface where the trapped men were. This would be a worrying sensation for most people anyway, but was made worse by the knowledge of the recent collapse of the pit roof. As Ian says in a letter home, 'It really was a wonderful sight the way the miners worked to extricate those two men, which they did in 7 hours, and I thought then when I saw them below that both would live.' They were brought out on a stretcher without needing amputation, but one of them died soon afterwards. The local papers reported the help given by the 'two heroic doctors', and we may be sure that it helped Ian's image in the St Helens area.

On a lighter note comes his introduction to first aid. This time it was an invitation to lecture to about 70 railwaymen on the subject for an unspecified fee. Ian cautiously agreed, aiming to slant the talk very much to anatomy and physiology, which filled his head at the time. Further discussion revealed that his predecessor hadn't charged any fee for the course, so Ian soon agreed to this too. However, on the next day he received a message that the head office in London would give him a first class rail pass for a year on the London, Midland, & Scottish Railway. This would include the whole area of London, Liverpool, Edinburgh and Belfast, so he felt that he had had a good bargain. More important in the long run was that it led to Ian's increasing involvement in first aid and the St John Ambulance Brigade when he returned home.

While he was at St Helens, in May 1926, he took a fortnight's course in the Hospital Necker in Paris costing £30, with lectures and access to cadavers and operative surgery. He described the high points in an article 60 years later, and while he would admit that he learnt something, it seems to have been an exercise in how to overcome difficulties that were mostly inflicted by the teacher. The *pièce de résistance* was when a pale, thin young man had a tuberculous kidney removed, the renal vessels being left clamped. The surgeon, Professor Legeu, then removed the clamp and in the torrential bleeding that ensued, simply packed the wound tightly, clipped the vessels one by one and closed up with the artery forceps still in position (Fraser, 1992). As a souvenir Ian brought back a signed photograph of the professor!

After his time at St Helens he took the second part of his FRCS of the Irish College in December 1926, again gaining first place in Ireland in each subject. He then returned to London for a course in the wards and operating theatres of Guy's Hospital from March to May 1927. As in the earlier period in London, this unpaid attachment gave him plenty of time to study. He followed this up in May by taking his Fellowship of the London College and in June 1927 by taking the MCh of Queen's University by examination (with Commendation). This catalogue of success indicates not only his academic brilliance but his capacity for sustained hard work. Mr Grant Massie of Guy's Hospital in a subsequent testimonial as glowing as that of Professor Yeates, commented that 'Mr Fraser's clinical abilities impressed me then in an unusual degree and I would put him among the first of the more outstanding candidates with whom I have come in contact during the past eight years.'

In spite of (and perhaps because of) his successes, Ian took a very cynical view of examinations. 'How can the pretty girl fail to make a better initial impression on a susceptible examiner than her spotty faced untidy competitor?' He describes his final fellowship viva in London. 'I was ushered behind the screen to examine a young woman. At the same moment a tray of tea and biscuits was put down in front of her. She was very polite but very definite.

> 'Sir, I have been examined so often this afternoon that I insist on having my tea now if you don't mind.' I explained to her that this was the most important moment of my life and that the tea was really a secondary consideration. She said 'I will answer any questions but will not be examined', and so for 20 minutes I had the best lecture, a real critique on the cervical rib, better than I had ever had from any professor. She told me that most of the candidates had missed the fact that she had one on the other side. She gave the differential diagnosis, she repeated to me all that had

been said by the previous candidates and the questions of the examiner; in fact I had a splendid time, and so when the final laying on of hands took place she did not need to do the full striptease that she had done so often for my predecessors. So thanks to some Indian tea and a co-operative lady I got my fellowship. (Fraser, 1989, p. 111)

Like many of Ian's stories this should probably be taken with a pinch of salt, for any examiner knows that you can't pass any final examination by luck alone. However, Ian's moral is clear – 'God helps those who help themselves' – and this he held to throughout his life. He didn't just accept what happened to him; he made things happen as best suited his career.

His European visit in 1927 was to the Allgemeines Krankenhaus in Vienna, but it doesn't seem to have been as colourful as the Paris course and he has left no record of his experiences there.

THE INFLUENCE OF ANDREW FULLERTON

Ian had worked as a student under Andrew Fullerton, who had in fact been appointed to the chair of surgery in 1923, the year of Ian's graduation. From the outset Andrew Fullerton had a strong influence on him. Ian tried to model his career on his mentor's, and in fact chance resulted in many similarities. Andrew had qualified in 1890, taken his FRCS (Ireland) in 1901 and then had a long period in the Royal Victoria Hospital as Assistant Surgeon (from 1902). When war broke out in 1914 the War Office asked the Royal Colleges of Surgeons to nominate surgeons for consultant posts as colonels in the RAMC. It required the great upheaval of the war to show his full potential and to ensure his upgrading to Attending Surgeon when he returned home.

Andrew Fullerton modelled himself on Robert Campbell and did an immense amount of surgery in the Out Patient Department. He brought to the hospital each day his hospital notes, a collection of several boxes of cystoscopes, a few books that might illustrate the case that he was going to operate on and, if the case needed diathermy, he brought from home his portable diathermy apparatus. This was a large and awkward box, which Ian carried frequently as a junior doctor; it seemed to weigh as much as a half-hundredweight bag of potatoes and was about as convenient to carry. One of his more cynical assistants said that instead of 'portable' it should be called 'shiftable'.

Although always interested in general surgery, Fullerton was a pioneer with the cystoscope and used to practise at night for hours putting the instrument through a small hole in a child's toy football. In time he could touch easily every part of the interior with the tip of a ureteric catheter. Again, this story has the rider that on one occasion he called over a colleague to look through the cystoscope into the bladder, saying 'Come here, I see a vessel' to which it is said that his colleague replied 'Is it my duty now to say 'Ship ahoy?'. This story, of course, reflects the usual Belfast distrust of any clever innovation.

One of Ian's appointments during his year as house surgeon was to Professor Andrew Fullerton's ward, and from his writings and Fullerton's reference they clearly had great respect for each other. Early in 1927 Ian returned to the ward as registrar and developed a new range of experience. The house surgeon or registrar was frequently asked to go with the surgeon to assist with the operation, give the anaesthetic, drive the car and help generally. Ian remembers:

> At the house itself I had to set the scene while my chief was upstairs seeing the patient, and I was responsible for getting the room suitably arranged down below – taking the flowers off the piano, making a good open space for the kitchen table; one did not do too much disturbing of furniture as this raised the dust, and there was usually a good deal of it available as the place had not been dusted for ages, if ever. I had to make sure there was free access to hand basins. From all this I learned a lot, and so when my time came to do this type of surgery I found it not too difficult . (I have happy memories of operating on a strangulated hernia in a cottage close to the water edge in a small seaside village. There was a knock at the window and I found it was an inquisitive hen wondering what was going on.) (Fraser, 1989, p. 16)

Domiciliary surgery sounds primitive, but it was the custom of the time. One has to remember that even George VI had his surgery for cancer of the lung at home. Much more hazardous was the practice of allowing the patient's general practitioner to give the anaesthetic, whether he had any competence in the task or not. Surgeons and house surgeons were more likely to be adequate as anaesthetists, but professional anaesthetists were very rare and the use of the term 'anaesthetic death' for any death on the operating table was not entirely unjustified. Ian knew this as well as any surgeon, and in his presidential address to the BMA (1962) he acknowledges that 'advances in anaesthesia have given new scope to surgery'. Having said all this and having sung the praises of the Ulster-born Sir Ivan Magill for his invention of the endotracheal tube, Ian always regarded anaesthetists as, at best, a necessary evil. As he says, the anaesthetic tubing allowed us 'to get the anaesthetist to take up his seat about three feet away and not clutter up the area of the operation' (Fraser, 1989, p. 86).

Andrew Fullerton held the chair in surgery until 1933, for which he was paid the princely sum of £500 per year. His university work consisted of bedside teaching on two or three mornings a week, an afternoon lecture at the university during term time and conducting the final MB exams twice a year. Ian was appointed as his assistant in the university duties in 1932, being paid £200 a year, and admits that this was gross overpayment for these duties. His main job was to call for the professor each day, take him to the university, install him in the lecture theatre and close the door. The only problem was that he always had to have a possible lecture in his pocket. On one occasion when Ian called with the professor he was asked what one should do for acute appendicitis. Ian replied 'operate at once', to which Fullerton replied 'That is what I am going to do, so will you please go and take my lecture.' The assistant's other job was to arrange suitable cases for the clinical examination. This was easy at the Royal Victoria and at the Mater Hospital, which cooperated readily, but the Infirmary (now Belfast City Hospital), having no great love for the Royal Victoria or University, often raised difficulties.

In 1931 the Association of Surgeons of Great Britain and Ireland came to Belfast and Professor Fullerton, president for the year, arranged a demonstration nephrectomy for their benefit, assisted by Ian. The visitors were all crowded into the theatre and Andrew was describing in detail the procedures: 'I am now freeing the posterior surface of the kidney. I am now freeing the anterior surface. I have now swept round the upper pole, and am now clearing the lower pole. I am now clearing the lower pole – clearing the lower pole.' After several more repetitions Ian had the temerity to whisper and ask what had gone wrong. To which the answer was 'Get rid of these b——rs. There is no lower pole: it's a horseshoe kidney'. The audience discreetly melted away and though Ian was not actually blamed, he certainly felt that as the assistant he should have selected a more straightforward case for the demonstration. The mistake was most unfortunate but diagnosis of this rare complication was much more difficult in the days before excretion urography.

On the final evening the president was giving, as was the custom then, a dinner to entertain the council and other VIPs. It was held in his own house, and Ian was invited to meet the 'greats' after a discreet enquiry as to whether he had a dinner jacket. After dinner Ian was sitting on a sofa beside one of the visitors and was asked if he was a member of the 'club' (i.e. the Association of Surgeons). Ian thought this a rather disrespectful term for such an important body but admitted that he was not. His neighbour then said he should join, and offered to put his name forward. Some time later in the evening, when the port had gone round twice, his interrogator repeated the same question and again offered to help. Indeed the process was repeated a second time, at which point Ian wrote his name on a piece of paper for the speaker. The paper was stuffed into the trouser pocket and, as Ian thought, forgotten about. No one was more surprised than Ian when four days later he received a letter to say that he had been elected. In fact it appeared that his neighbour at the dinner had been the secretary of the Association, 'Joey' Hughes of Guy's Hospital, who had simply added his name to the list of members. Subsequently some of the presidents made sure that admission was a much more formal process, and Ian felt that he had managed to gain admission by the 'tradesman's entrance'.

Ian worked with Andrew Fullerton for most of the next ten years and developed a strong admiration for him. In later life he wrote no fewer than six articles discussing his contribution to surgery. The first, on 'Great teachers of surgery in the past' (1964), is the most detailed. Ian describes how 'his enthusiasm pervaded the ward' and 'his own integrity and his example produced a loyalty now rarely seen'. 'His ward rounds were crowded. There were many anecdotes and incidents recounted from his war service in France that all helped to make his clinics well attended and well remembered.' In due course Fullerton was elected president of the Royal College of Surgeons in Ireland (the first president from Ulster) and president of the Association of Surgeons. The parallels with Ian's career appear again and again. Only with regard to the Chair of Surgery did Ian fail to follow his mentor, as we shall see. Fullerton retired in 1933 aged 65, and died in the following year. A few hours after his death the chauffeur drove up to Ian's door with some boxes of cystoscopes, some books and, laid across the top, the fellowship gown of the Royal College of Surgeons in Ireland. Ian was to wear it on all suitable occasions in memory of this outstanding man, great teacher and close personal friend.

APPOINTMENT TO THE CHILDREN'S HOSPITAL

One day in the autumn of 1926 Ian was preparing to assist at an operation in the Royal Victoria Hospital when Andrew Fullerton said 'I am President of the Royal College of Surgeons in Ireland, Professor of Surgery at Queen's University, Belfast, and visiting surgeon at the Royal Victoria Hospital and the Hospital for Sick Children. I am going to give up something and it will be my appointment to the Children's Hospital – you must apply, but you will not get it.' Ian did apply, and after three weeks of intensive canvassing was appointed (as honorary assistant surgeon to the outpatient department, a post that he held until 1945), beating off stiff competition from C.J.A. 'Cocky' Woodside.

The method of appointment to posts has changed so much in the past 20 years that it is worth reminding ourselves how it was in the 1920s and 1930s, and even into the 1960s. First, one had to obtain testimonials from one's teachers, which were open and of little discriminatory value. Nevertheless, the conscientious members of the RVH staff must have spent hours writing these for all their students. As we have seen, Ian never misses a chance of a dig at Surgeon Kirk, whose basic testimonial apparently read 'Dr A. B. has qualified MB BCh. I am very glad, T.S. Kirk'. Copies of these testimonials had to be printed in a little application book for the medical staff posts (many of which survive in the RVH Office of Archives). The candidate then had to go round all the members of the hospital board canvassing for himself. Ian comments: 'I found that canvassing was unpleasant, and I thought it should not be necessary, but everyone did it, and I am told that all the members of the Board, if they had not been approached, felt they had been overlooked' (Fraser, 1993). Having said this, he also comments. 'I look back on these visits now with great pleasure', which is more believable, knowing Ian's outgoing nature and ability to talk to anyone.

> I remember one of two of them very well. I remember visiting a very wealthy lady in the Malone area and having afternoon tea in her elegant drawing room. I sat on the sofa and remembered to cock my little finger at the right angle as I sipped my tea. All went well until she asked me the colour of the cushion beside me on the sofa. I said 'brown, yellow and green'. This did not please her – I should have known the colours were those that her jockey wore at all races on all occasions. I am afraid I got no marks and I never knew whether she supported me or not. Next day my visit was a very different one. I called at a small house on the Newtownards Road to interview a shipyard worker, a very valuable member of the Working Men's Committee. The door was very long in being opened by his wife, explaining that she had to take her rubber apron off because she had been working at the jaw box (kitchen sink). She said himself would not be in until 5.30 p.m. but he would be 'washed up' by six o'clock and ready to see me. So I came back and enjoyed my half hour with him. Sadly I did not know enough about Association football or of Linfield's chances of winning the cup. Had it been rugby I think I could have held my own. One other visit that I remember very well was to my neighbour Mr Hugh C. Kelly. He had played rugby for Ireland, lacrosse for Ireland and he was an international golfer. I was most intrigued when he told me that as a member of the Royal Ulster Club he had sailed on the *American Contender* [*sic*] – I suppose as a spy to see that no illegal incidents took place. Hugh C. Kelly and his wife (I later found that her name was Ethel, which explains why they called their house Hecklands) went everywhere on bicycles, always with a small mongrel dog which followed closely at their heels. I remember one of these dogs was called Sieben – he had been given by him to his wife on their seventh wedding anniversary. Another dog that he had was called Tanner because he had bought it for sixpence at the dogs' home. His window overlooked our garden and I remember him knocking on the window one day when I was kicking a football and telling me to stop at once and he would come down to show me how to kick it

correctly, which he did. I improved so much that later I kicked the ball over the hedge cracking one of his windows. I remember going cap in hand to apologise, but instead of being cross and unpleasant he congratulated me on how much my kicking had improved. He naturally to me was a great man. I look back on those visits with great pleasure. (Fraser, 1993, p. 3)

The object of the canvassing was, of course, to make oneself known to the Board member, who would ask what did your father do, what school did you go to, what games did you play, and of course a rugby international cap was better than first-class honours or an FRCS. All these preliminaries shortened the actual interview when the time came, for the members had all made up their minds beforehand!

The Children's Hospital was then in Queen Street and Ian had in fact never worked there, or even visited it. Clinical practice on his arrival there has been vividly portrayed by Ian in his Robert Campbell Memorial Oration (Fraser, 1973). The matron was all-powerful because she carried such a wide responsibility within the hospital, as anaesthetist, dentist, catering and general manager and, of course, nurse. Anaesthesia consisted of asphyxia plus ether from the Clover inhaler. The surgeon was often single-handed or had only help from a junior nurse. The nurses in their spare time repaired surgical gloves, rolled gauze bandages, made up plaster-of-Paris bandages and prepared catgut, both plain and chromic. The hospital had no X-ray machine until 1932, the outpatient department was a sort of glass annexe like a greenhouse, with the special smell of unwashed mother and incontinent child – and there were fleas and lice. In stark contrast to all this was the office of the chairman of the Management Committee, which was elegantly furnished and never used. Life was not all work in the Children's Hospital, and on several occasions Ian figured as Santa Claus at Christmas.

Senior surgical appointments at that time were usually for life, unless one committed some heinous crime or was incapacitated, and Ian did indeed hold the post until 1945 and was attending surgeon until his overall retirement in 1966. Like other such posts it was unpaid until 1948 and the duties were not specified in detail. However, it was essentially to see outpatients and carry out such operations as were thought necessary, in conjunction with other staff. Unfortunately, at that time appointment to the Children's

Hospital staff was regarded merely as a stepping-stone to a more prestigious appointment elsewhere. Members of the staff therefore tended to reduce their commitment when they were appointed to the staff of the Royal Victoria Hospital and at any time there was always a junior staff surgeon carrying out most of the work and one or more senior surgeons with primary duties elsewhere.

SURGERY AND RELATED ACTIVITIES OF THE 1930S

Ian continued with his duties as clinical assistant to Professor Fullerton and subsequently to Professor Crymble, and was registrar to the Dental Department in the Royal Victoria Hospital 1932–4. However, with his high attainments he was naturally aiming for a post as honorary assistant surgeon in the Royal Victoria Hospital and resisted the temptation to apply for a post in a provincial hospital. He made various applications during the 1930s but without success, seeing Barney Purce appointed in 1930, C.J.A. 'Cocky' Woodside in 1933 and Cecil Calvert in 1935. This was fair on grounds of age and seniority of medical qualification (and Barney Purce and 'Cocky' Woodside had been in the RAMC during the First World War), but must have been galling for an ambitious young man.

In theory he had no beds and only outpatient clinics in the Royal Victoria Hospital, so he had to concentrate on his work in the Children's Hospital and try to build up his private practice somehow. In fact he was given about four out of the 50 beds in a double ward at the Royal Victoria Hospital. He calculated that in one typical week he did 28 operations in Belfast, 24 of which were in hospital and unpaid and four in nursing homes. At that time there were 20 or 30 nursing homes in Belfast, each with an operating theatre and boiling water sterilizer but no surgical instruments, so that each surgeon had to bring his own. The Musgrave clinic was not opened until 1938 and the Clark wing was added after the Second World War; they offered much better facilities for middle-income patients. In addition, Ian carried out some operations for general practitioners in the country and even a few on Saturdays in London. The latter were arranged by his near contemporary from Queen's, R. Leslie Dodds FRCS, who was now an established gynaecologist in Harley Street. The two had met frequently when Ian was at the course in the

Middlesex Hospital, and had obtained the English Fellowship in the same year.

By and large the relationship between the junior and his chief in the ward was very satisfactory. The amount of work that the junior was allowed to do depended on how busy the chief was and how much trust he could put in his registrar. On the other hand the chief was remarkably regular with his ward rounds. There was much less work in the Law Courts than in more recent times to provide a regular temptation. Certainly the chief's hospital attendance was better than in London, where the story is told of a lady who went into hospital and came out after three weeks cured and well satisfied. So she went round to Harley Street to thank the surgeon, commenting in passing that she had never actually seen him in the ward. To which the surgeon replied 'Madam, do you go to church?' 'Yes', she said, and received the reply 'And do you expect to see God?'

Apart from employing his skill as a surgeon, publication of surgical papers was a feature of this period and altogether there were a surprising number, 24 between 1930 and 1939 (see Appendix 1). Most of them are case reports or reviews of aspects of surgery, such as cancer of the mouth (1930) or diverticulitis of the colon (1932). The latter topic was part of his MD thesis, which he submitted successfully to Queen's University in December 1932 (*Causes, pathology and treatment of diverticula of the small and large intestine*). The last of his academic distinctions in the pre-war era was his election to honorary Fellowship of the Royal Society of Edinburgh, an honour that requires the support of at least four Fellows, in 1939. This was followed by the admission to fellowship of the American College of Surgeons in 1940.

One of the sidelines for the junior surgeon in earning a living was in 'grinding', i.e. coaching undergraduates for their forthcoming exams. Ian took over this surgical 'grind' from R.J. McConnell and remained a superb teacher throughout his life. He gave the lectures and tutorials in an old empty room in the UVF hospital at the back of Queen's. Already in the 1930s he was able to attract a regular following prepared to pay for sound clinical teaching coupled with the equally essential knowledge of the examiners' quirks and obsessions.

We have seen that Ian's experience in Lancashire gave him an interest in first aid. This took on a practical form when, in 1931, he accepted the appointment of Divisional Surgeon to the Belfast Division of the St John Ambulance Brigade. This was associated with the York Street Railway Station (LMS NCC) and he ran first aid classes in the First Class Waiting Room there. He was appointed joint honorary secretary to the Northern Ireland District in 1931. The time was plainly ripe and such was his energy that between 1932 and 1939, while he was District Commissioner, the numbers increased from three Divisions and 138 members to 63 Divisions and 1,944 members. The post involved overall responsibility for teaching and training, and competitions for quality of first aid etc. There were, of course, many other doctors involved, including his friends Dr Victor Fielden and Dr Bill Strain. Even by early in 1938 there was the additional pressure of impending war, with air raid precautions and decontamination drill under way. Ian was admitted to the Order of St John as a Commander (Brother) in 1935, and in 1940, when he was already away on active service, he was awarded the OBE (Civilian Division) for his work with the Order of St John, followed by promotion to Knight of Grace in 1941.

One of Ian's outside activities was to be Chief Medical Officer for the Ards TT car race. This was one of the great occasions in the inter-war years, and an account in a motoring magazine describes the dedication of more than 200 doctors and qualified Red Cross nurses and men-workers scattered round the course, along with seven or eight 'motor ambulances'. 'The entire organization is controlled by Mr Ian Fraser, the Chief Medical Officer, whose problem it is to ensure that at whatever spot on the thirteen miles course an accident may happen the injured may have immediate medical attention, and be sent to hospital if need be … During the race Mr Fraser himself remains at the control office opposite the pits, where he is in touch by telephone with the zone control posts at Bradshaw's Brae, Newtownards, The Moat, Comber, Ballystockart and Dundonald Corner, and on receipt of notification of an accident on any part of the course, can hasten to the scene if necessary' (*Monthly Review*). The TT races started in 1928 and continued until 1936, when Jack Chambers crashed into a lamp post in Newtownards, killing eight spectators and injuring 15 others. Ian was the Chief Medical Officer for every race except the 1928 event.

He examined for the Fellowship of the Royal College of Surgeons in Ireland 1937–9, establishing the links with the college that were to lead eventually to his presidency.

Ian's other medical honour in this period was his election as president of the Belfast Medical Students' Association for 1938–9. For this he gave a presidential address on the subject of 'Foreign bodies', a subject on which he ranged from the serious to the bizarre, to the entertaining. The highlight of the year was a weekend in London (9–13 February 1939), visiting the Middlesex and Great Ormond Street Hospitals, the Royal College of Surgeons, the BBC and the Ireland–England rugby match at Twickenham. Ian had taken the precaution of asking the Royal Ulster Constabulary in Belfast for a letter of support to take with him in case of trouble. The letter read 'Doctor Ian Frazer [sic] is well known to the police in Belfast. He is taking a group of 25 to 30 Medical Students to London on Thursday, 9th instant, returning on the 12th instant. The purpose of the visit is to see the London Hospitals and the Ireland and England Rugby Match. R.D. Harrison, Commissioner of Police'. The match was bound to be exciting, but no one could have predicted that Dr Sinclair Irwin (later FRCS) would score the winning try just in front of the BMSA party. Sinclair was son of Ian's old teacher Sir Samuel Irwin and was soon to join the army and to be incarcerated in a German POW camp for most of the war, before returning to be consultant surgeon at the Royal Victoria Hospital. In the event the students created no trouble and returned home highly pleased with the trip.

SURGICAL TRAVELLING

By 1937 Ian was sufficiently senior to be invited to join one of the surgical clubs, in his case the Surgical Travellers, chaired at the time by Mr W. Heneage Ogilvie. There were many of these clubs in the United Kingdom with about 25 members in each, members being from similar fields but above all amiable, enthusiastic, interested and interesting. This number meant that three groups of eight could watch surgeons at work and even when all the wives where present at social functions, numbers were acceptable. Ian went with the Surgical Travellers to Vienna and Budapest in 1938, and indeed it was an ominous year in which to visit Austria. They went out by the Golden Arrow Train to Vienna, and checked in to the Hotel Bristol on the Ringstrasse. They then unpacked and joined the others for dinner and chat. On the following day the men set off for the first of their hospital visits – to the Algemeine Krankenhaus. When they returned to their hotel an embarrassed hotel porter told them that regrettably they had been moved to another hotel, which he said was just as good. Ian protested that they had booked six months earlier, etc., etc., but there was nothing to be done and they had to accept the move. Only the next day did they discover from the newspapers that Von Papen, the German Chancellor, had arrived in Austria and taken over the hotel lock, stock and barrel.

They saw all the great names of the city at that time; Denk and Ranzi, the two professors of Vienna, each with about 200 beds and ten assistants in their clinics, but only they were allowed to carry on private practice. They also saw Böhler of the Böhler splint and Finsterer, who was clearly outside the establishment and worked in poor, cramped conditions. The Krankenhaus, which included many separate clinics, had a shop where one was expected to purchase photographs of the chief surgeons, which could then be signed personally.

They spent four days in Vienna before moving on by bus to Budapest. There they saw surgery that was perhaps better than in Vienna and met Professor Von Lichtenberg, the inventor of the technique of intravenous pyelography. As a Jew he had been driven out of Germany and soon after their visit was to move on to South America. All in all, it was an instructive visit highlighting not only the depressed state of Vienna after the dismemberment of its old empire, but the precipice on which all Europe rested before Germany gave it one further push.

In September 1938 they attended the 11th International Congress of Surgery in Brussels, one of the last such events before the outbreak of war. These congresses were run triennially by the International Society for Surgery, and this one had been originally planned for Vienna, but the political situation necessitated the move to Brussels at short notice. It was a lavish affair with over 500 delegates, but they must have been on edge with Chamberlain capitulating to Germany in Munich and Churchill's forebodings of war proving all too true.

Surprisingly many previous congresses had been beset with trouble, ranging from shouts of *A bas les Anglais* in Cairo in 1932 to a bullet in the nose for Mussolini in Rome in 1929.

MARRIAGE AND FAMILY LIFE

Ian continued to live mainly at home during the 1920s, when he was not resident in hospital or away on courses. His private practice from about 1928 was carried out from rooms in University Square that he shared with the surgeon Harry Malcolm, as guests of his dentist cousin, Marshall Swan. For relaxation, his main interests were playing bridge with friends such as Dr Maurice Wilson, the neurologist, and listening to music, particularly Gilbert and Sullivan light opera. He took a keen interest in the rugby internationals and managed to get to the matches at Twickenham, Lansdowne Road and Paris fairly regularly. As we have seen, he gave up rugby at Queen's but continued with hockey until after qualification. At this stage, like so many doctors, he took up golf, first at Scrabo and later at Malone. When on holiday on the north coast he played frequently at Dunfanaghy and Ballycastle.

By the 1930s Ian was at least partly established on the ladder with his 'attending' post in the Children's Hospital, even if he did not yet have his post in the Royal Victoria Hospital. The next landmark for Ian was therefore his marriage on 2 September 1931 in Fitzroy Presbyterian Church to Eleanor Margaret Mitchell. She was the elder daughter of Marcus A. Mitchell of Quarry House, Strandtown, and Alice Jane Cuthbert. Alice Jane was in fact a first cousin of Ian's stepmother, and Ian and Eleanor had known each other since childhood. They immediately bought 33 Wellington Park and this house remained their home (apart from the war years) until 1952. The family worshipped in Fitzroy Presbyterian Church, which was within easy walking distance behind Queen's University. Ian and Eleanor were regular attenders for most of their lives, but certainly Ian had more relaxed views on religion than his father.

Their first child, John Colin Cuthbert Fraser, was born on 25 December 1935 at 33 Wellington Park, but he died on 13 February 1938 from tuberculous meningitis. The next child, Mary Alice Fraser, was born on 4 April 1938 and at this stage Una Davidson came into the house as a nurse and remained a close family friend for the rest of her long life. Their third child and only surviving son, Ian Marcus Moore Fraser, was born on 12 November 1939, by which time Britain was at war and Ian was awaiting call-up with the RAMC.

The busy routine of Ian's life, engaged in private practice when it came his way, operating in nursing homes and private houses and seeing private patients at home on Saturday mornings, has already been touched on. As well as the nurse for the children, the family always had a resident cook and parlour maid but, while it might seem to us now that life would be completely idle, the absence of labour-saving machines and supermarkets meant that there was more than enough to fill the day. Eleanor was occupied like many other wives of the period with shopping, entertaining, flower arranging and jam making, as well as gardening, organizing picnics and playing badminton.

The family also managed to have fairly ambitious summer holidays, getting out of Ireland every year to Cornwall, Scotland, Germany, Belgium and Yorkshire. In many cases medical meetings provided a starting point for a few days' holiday, the trip to Belgium proving particularly memorable. It was a full and satisfying pattern of life, soon to be rudely shattered by the outbreak of war.

Chapter 4

The Second World War – service in a backwater

WAR DECLARED

War was declared against Germany on 3 September 1939 and this was to take Ian away from his seemingly endless role as Clinical Assistant in the Royal Victoria Hospital to a field where he could show his organizational abilities. Naturally, like most of his contemporaries, he volunteered for service in the army, though he was not immediately called up. There was conscription in Great Britain but not in Northern Ireland, and of those who enrolled only regulars and territorials were involved immediately.

The first news of actual call-up that Ian heard was in late October when he was on his way to an outpatient session in the Children's Hospital. He was stopped by Dr Fred Allen (later professor of paediatrics), who was the local link with the War Office. He was told that a surgeon was urgently required and his name had come up. Ian told his informant that it was a very awkward time as his wife was going to have a baby in two weeks' time and he wanted to be at home to help. He received the unsympathetic reply 'Do you expect the war to stop to see you through your problem?' There was no answer to that, but later the same day a piece of luck arrived in that Dr Alfred Turner from his own year, who had gone to Persia with what became the Anglo-Iranian Oil Company, suddenly decided that he would like to come home to join up. He had an FRCS and was eligible, so Dr Allen phoned the War Office offering this replacement. It was agreed, and Ian remained at home for a few weeks more. Marcus Fraser was born on 12 November. Ian later found out that the

40

substitute surgeon had spent two miserable years in Madagascar, but they came together again in Catania in 1943.

During the first three months of the war Ian therefore continued with his usual work in the Royal Victoria and Belfast Children's Hospitals, together with his struggling private practice. In December he was summoned for a medical examination prior to being accepted into the RAMC. He was interviewed by the Assistant Director of Medical Services (ADMS), a retired RAMC colonel who claimed that he had been the youngest ADMS in the First World War and now was the oldest in the Second World War. He intended to carry out a medical examination, but there was no stethoscope and no blood pressure apparatus. He was lucky to find some coloured wool in a drawer, and when Ian was able to distinguish red from green his medical examination ended and he was given his commission, immediately upgraded to major.

Stranmillis Teacher Training College had been commandeered as a hospital with Lieutenant-Colonel Dan McVicker, a retired regular soldier, as commanding officer, Ian as medical officer in charge of the surgical section and his contemporary, Dr T.H. Crozier, on the medical side. Ian was posted there in February 1940 and by June Northern Ireland was flooded with troops that had returned from Dunkirk. They had come partly to spread the armed forces over the UK but also to be in an area reasonably safe from bombing. With the troops came four general hospitals, which also had to be accommodated in the Belfast area. Space was found finally in Campbell College, whose boys were evacuated to Portrush. A second hospital went to a school in Bangor, a third took over Musgrave Park Hospital, and the fourth remained mobile with trucks hidden under trees and the officers camped on very muddy land at Whiteabbey. These hospitals were staffed by highly qualified specialists who had nothing very taxing to do, and an arrangement was soon built up by which some of them took over a surgical list from Ian in Stranmillis on one day a week.

When Ian was first called up he heard by the 'grapevine' that he was to be posted to Finland, so, having found out that Finland was a pretty cold place, he rapidly equipped himself with a pair of 'drawers woollen long' (DWL). After some months this proved to be a typical wartime rumour, and the intended posting was changed to

West Africa. The DWL were then banished to the attic and eventually to 'War on Want', while he supplied himself with shorts and a topi. West Africa was not of course an area of combat but since Germany and Italy controlled the Mediterranean, control of the south Atlantic was necessary to ensure the safety of our ships heading round the Cape. (The Vichy French by this time provided Germany with submarine bases in various parts of French West Africa.) The importance of this sea channel at that time was to allow Britain to build up an army in Egypt prior to launching the North African front. In fact, all three services were involved in the route and planes were shipped in crates to the Gold Coast, assembled and then flown across Africa to Egypt.

JOURNEY TO WEST AFRICA

After delays because of a rumoured German invasion of Ireland, Ian was given the new posting to the 37th General Hospital, with 1,000 beds, which was first built up at Gillingham, Dorset. There wasn't too much to do and at least it was possible for Eleanor to come over to Gillingham with him. Ian was in charge of the Surgical Division and was promoted to lieutenant-colonel. On 7 May 1941, on board the *Highland Princess* from Liverpool, they set off for Accra in the Gold Coast. This sort of sea journey, described by Ian in a detailed diary that has survived, was by no means a pleasure cruise at that time. There were air raids on Liverpool docks before they left and ships were frequently being torpedoed. However, the mixed convoy of three ships carrying troops, weapons and freight had an escort of a cruiser and four destroyers and, although there were frequent alarms, they were not attacked. After initial concerns about boat drill and how to evacuate patients if required, they settled down to a regime of keeping fit, balanced by reading and bridge. Medical duties on the ship were light, but included treatment of scabies and malaria and checking on the TAB (typhoid and antityphoid) inoculation of the troops. One advantage of the quiet trip was that the medical team, with Colonel John McFadden as its commanding officer, got to know each other. He was an older brother of George McFadden FRCS, surgeon at the Belfast Infirmary (City Hospital).

The journey took them by a tortuous course from Liverpool

towards Iceland and down through the mid-Atlantic, docking first at Freetown (Sierra Leone) on 24 May. There they let off some 200 troops and naval personnel and took on stores. While there they heard of the tragic sinking of HMS *Hood* by the *Bismarck*, with the loss of almost all hands. This was followed a few days later by the destruction of the *Bismarck*. They also met survivors from many other sinkings off the African Coast – a reminder of how lucky they had been.

Freetown was clearly an important port, since they saw HMS *Renown* (battleship) and HMS *Eagle* (aircraft carrier) and many smaller ships. While there they visited hospitals, encountered some of the arguments as to prevention of malaria and met Dr Tom Davey, a Belfast graduate (MB 1925) and his wife. They were very hospitable in a beautiful house overlooking the bay, although Tom was struggling to recover from various unpleasant infections including typhus. He was to become Professor of Tropical Medicine at Liverpool after the war.

They steamed out of Freetown on 26 May, the weather becoming even hotter and more humid. Ian comments that they now had two ladies on board and all had to wear bathing suits in the pool on deck! They were now heading eastwards and on 30 May reached Takoradi, which was the main port of the Gold Coast since Accra had a poor harbour. The train journey involved a long detour via Kumasi (about 450 miles), and it was late on 1 June when they reached their destination.

THE GOLD COAST

The first task was to help set up the new 37th General Hospital with the Deputy Director of Medical Services (DDMS), Colonel Price, and the ADMS, Colonel Chandler, who were already there. The 1,000-bed hospital was planned with 200 beds for Europeans and 800 beds for Africans. Unfortunately, most of their equipment (gowns, gloves and surgical instruments) had come out separately and been lost in transit, leaving them with only a minor operating kit. Most difficulty was caused by the X-ray machine, which had been salvaged but gave constant trouble because of the exposure to salt water. The absence of gloves also caused trouble when one of the junior doctors was operating under local anaesthetic on a large penile ulcer of uncertain cause. At the end of the operation he pricked his finger with a needle and although the wound seemed entirely superficial and he washed it thoroughly, he eventually developed a sore on the spot that proved to be syphilitic. After energetic treatment with the remedies available at the time he appeared to make a full recovery before returning home. However, he later developed cardiac problems which the War Office accepted as syphilitic, and it granted him an army pension.

While Ian was helping to arrange quarters on their first day, a party of junior officers went down to the beach. Shortly afterwards they got news in the hospital of a tragedy there and they rushed down and found that two of the officers had got into difficulties in the water; one had survived and after artificial respiration was taken safely to the European Hospital, but Major Woodruff, who all knew to be an excellent swimmer, could not be resuscitated. By the time Ian arrived it was clearly time to give up artificial respiration, so Ian had the sad task of arranging for the funeral on the next day. He also arranged for a telegram to be sent off at first-class rate to tell Woodruff's recently married wife that he had been drowned. To compound the pathos of the situation, Woodruff had already dispatched a telegram at second-class rate saying that he had arrived safely, so Ian had yet another task a month later in writing to explain the muddle when the second telegram arrived before the first.

A group of 25 QA nursing sisters (Queen Alexandra's Imperial Military Nursing Service) had been posted to Accra along with the new medical team, but in the event set off from England ten days later. Unfortunately, they had a much less pleasant trip than Ian, for they were bombed soon after leaving Liverpool (without serious damage) and were torpedoed near Freetown. Fortunately, the ship went down slowly and all the sisters escaped in the lifeboats, though their kit was lost. Only one of the sisters was in uniform at the time and wearing her Queen Alexandra silver badge on her lapel. All the others were in evening dress, as the Captain had told them they were in safe waters and could relax. One of the benefits of the Gold Coast economy was that they had plenty of silver and, using a cuttlefish as a mould, they were soon able to make replica badges, which, although crude, became much prized. New uniforms for the nurses were easily obtained, but they had no working shoes. Ian remembered his Cuthbert cousins in South Africa, who had a large leather company, and a request for help produced a consignment of shoes as a present and several boxes of chocolates.

Almost immediately it became apparent that the military hospital would probably not be busy since there was no fighting in the area and the soldiers were essentially young and fit. The doctors therefore had to fill in their time usefully, and set out to broaden their skills with tropical diseases and problems of women and children. They therefore soon developed a good relationship with both the African and the European hospitals, where they were able to see and operate on a wide range of diseases. These included guinea worms, tropical sores, deep muscle abscess, elephantiasis of the scrotum, yaws and vesico-vaginal fistulae. The last of these resulted from the problems of female circumcision causing vaginal stenosis, and obstructed labour. A ureteric transplant into the colon was the standard operation. Trauma was common from road accidents since the Africans were not always competent drivers. On the other hand, cancer of the breast and appendicitis were very rare.

On one occasion when sitting down to dinner, Ian was called suddenly to the telephone to be told that a surgical specialist was requested urgently for a young naval officer who had been badly burnt. Ian flew to Takoradi and found this man with a badly burnt face, eyes closed and totally unrecognizable. When they began to talk they realized that they were old friends: this was J. Osborne King, later to become a prominent estate agent in Belfast. The results of Ian's surgery were fairly satisfactory, apart from one ear that was more severely damaged, and they continued to meet long after the war.

In February 1942 Singapore fell to the Japanese. Apart from its many disastrous consequences to those involved, this meant the loss of two important commodities to the wider world – quinine and rubber. The absence of quinine had serious consequences for the troops in Africa since mepacrine, the best synthetic alternative, was not freely available. When it did arrive it was unpopular and soldiers refused to take it because it made them yellow, and allegedly made them 'less amorous'. It must be said that some of the doctors had refused to take even quinine, for no very clear reason. Ian, like so many others, had several attacks of malaria but fortunately was eventually able to overcome the recurrent infection.

Loss of the rubber supplies meant that there was a shortage of rubber gloves and the War Office asked senior surgeons to carry out an interesting experiment. They were asked to operate for one week doing a full list with bare hands. Ian found this very distressing but did go through with it (apart for one case involving a knee joint which he postponed). The worry, of course was not only the surgeon's hygiene but also that of the sister and assistant. In the event nothing went wrong with any of the cases.

By May 1942 Ian had been recognized as unofficial adviser to the DDMS on surgical questions, and in December of that year he was appointed consulting surgeon to the West Africa command (Gambia, Sierra Leone, the Gold Coast and Nigeria) with the rank of colonel. It was designated 'temporary' as all officers' ranks were during wartime. Although the four colonies were close together, they were separated by strips of territory controlled by Vichy France. Even with communication by air, a lot of time was spent in travelling as it was always necessary to fly out to sea in a wide detour. Not all French territories were under Vichy control, and the large territory then called Equatorial Africa, and now Chad, was controlled by a black governor loyal to de Gaulle. Accra was the seat of the Free French Mission for the whole of West Africa and there was close contact between the British surgeons there and Robert Jobez, originally from Paris, a diplomat with the Free French Mission. Ian became close friends with Robert Jobez and Thérèse, both then and later, a friendship helped by a mutual fondness for bridge, and visited them at Meudon, near Paris.

RELAXATION

Life in Accra was not all work, and the army doctors must have been pretty tired of each other's company after a year and a half. They slept in small rooms on camp beds that had been brought out with them. These too became increasingly small and uncomfortable, even apart from the need for careful arrangement of the mosquito net, with a sheet or nothing for bedclothes. They dined in the officers' mess and Ian comments that the food was quite good. It had to be fresh, as meat and fish could not be kept. They couldn't grow potatoes, so they obtained their carbohydrates from the yam.

There was a wide range of tropical fruits – papaw, avocado and bananas at a penny a bunch – all much less common in Britain before the war than they are now. All citrus fruits were available and they saw a citrus farm where, with skilled grafting, all could even be grown on one tree. Their favourite drink in the mess was achimota, a fresh fruit drink made of oranges, lemons, limes and mandarins, all squeezed together. It also had to be drunk immediately or it would ferment.

They had frequent parties in the mess, which included the sisters, and were invited out about once a week by some of the expatriates. On these occasions they usually played bridge, held impromptu concerts or watched films. Outdoor activity included looking at the wildlife, especially the birds, and trying to understand the social customs and folklore of the local tribes. They played a variety of games according to skills, though the hard ground made the golf balls travel unnaturally far. Unfortunately Ian's detailed diary, like so many, was abandoned after the first two months, but we must imagine that the novelty of such an existence soon wore off and that leave was very welcome.

HOME ON LEAVE

Ian was eventually given leave in January 1943, and would normally have expected to return to the United Kingdom by the slow and dangerous sea journey. However, he had helped the Americans, who had no medical arrangements for their troops in the area, and it was not difficult to persuade them to take him as a passenger on one of their planes home. He was described as an 'overload' on the plane, but was assured that if the plane got off the ground, it would soon burn up the fuel equivalent to his extra weight.

On arrival in London he called to see the Director of Surgery, who said that he could now go home but that they would then like him to return to West Africa. Ian pointed out that this would be foolish as there was no work to be done there and he had seen no action, but that the North African campaign was well under way and he could do something useful there. This was agreed but he would have to revert to the rank of lieutenant-colonel; and so at last he returned to his wife and family in Belfast.

When Ian went away in 1940 Eleanor had let the house in Wellington Park and lived with the children and their nurse in Newcastle, County Down. At first they stayed in the Slieve Donard Hotel but soon moved to 4 The Downs, Newcastle. By the time Ian got leave Mary Alice would have been nearly five and Mark three and a half. He had missed the fun of seeing them as toddlers, and had all too little time to get to know them now.

Ian had been supplied with a ration book before he left the Gold Coast, but when he reached home he saw a notice in the daily paper saying that soldiers on leave might apply for petrol coupons, which would at least enable the family to travel a few hundred miles and visit friends in the country. So he immediately applied at a recruiting centre and got the necessary coupons. All went well until the young man asked for details of his car. He explained that his own car was on blocks in the garage with the water and oil drained off, and no batteries, but that his elderly father had kindly offered to lend him his car and return to the bicycle. At this the officious young man took back the coupons and tore them up saying 'a clever dodge, trying to fill the old man's car with petrol'. Ian was naturally furious but soon met an old friend who told him to cool down and think calmly. He should go to his father and ask him to make Ian a present of the car for two weeks. This he did and returned to the unpleasant young man who said 'What car is it now?'. Ian was able to say it was the same car but he had a formal piece of paper which said 'I Robert Moore Fraser, give my motor car, XYZ, to my son Ian Fraser'. At the end of two weeks Ian wrote a similar note saying 'I, Ian Fraser, give my motor car, XYZ, to my father Robert Moore Fraser'. Whether this was correct legally, he did not know, but it satisfied the bureaucrats.

Chapter 5

Penicillin – North Africa and Italy

INTRODUCTION TO PENICILLIN

Ian had had only had two or three weeks' leave when he was suddenly called to the War Office for an urgent consultation. They had received a new drug that had been experimentally used for some time in Oxford, and now the entire British stock of the drug was to be given to the army to be tried in the battlefield. It was called penicillin. Ian had never heard of it, but was told that he was now to become the army's expert on the drug. It was decided that he should go to Oxford to be fully trained under Professor Howard Florey. Although his leave was short, at least Eleanor was able to come over to Oxford with him, leaving the children in Newcastle with Una Davidson. They stayed in the usual university digs and life was not easy. In fact, they had to change three times as there was virtually no accommodation in the city.

The anti-bacterial action of the mould *Penicillium notatum* had been observed as far back as 1928 by Alexander Fleming in St Mary's Hospital, London, but he was never interested in administering any extract of the mould to animals or patients. This was left to Howard Florey, Professor of Pathology in Oxford, who was looking at various anti-bacterial substances with a colleague, Ernst Chain. They began work in the late 1930s and by 1939 had grants from both American and British sources to press ahead with the work. The next problem was to produce enough of the extract, and when they showed it to be effective against staphylococcal septicaemia in mice in May 1940, producing adequate supplies became more urgent still. They set up their own plant in the pathology laboratory at Oxford and had enough to test it in patients by February 1941.

During 1942 they persuaded pharmaceutical companies in

Britain and America to move into commercial production and, as the year went on, Florey's first wife, Dr Ethel Florey, treated more and more patients, confirming the real value of the extract (which still consisted of 90 per cent impurities). Two-thirds of the penicillin administered was excreted in the urine, and such was the scarcity of penicillin that the urine of patients treated was collected by Dr Florey, cycling round Oxford, and the penicillin extracted from it. (Dr Florey's journeys were referred to as 'The Morning Milk Round' or 'The P Patrol'). Ironically, this form of penicillin contained fewer impurities than the original preparation, and was often referred to as policeman's penicillin, after the first patient to receive the new drug. It was found in clinical use to cause much less pain on injection than the original, rather impure form, which looked like mustard and felt like it on injection!

This was the stage at which Ian was sent to Oxford for a month to hear about clinical findings so far and to plan for its use on battle casualties. It was agreed that since Florey had carried out trials on osteomyelitis, bacterial endocarditis and venereal disease, the RAMC trial should concentrate on trauma. In fact, they later bent the rules over a nursing sister who developed salpingitis, probably gonorrhoeal, and found penicillin to be very effective. The Americans had plentiful supplies and used it routinely for venereal disease. It was also suggested that the scarce drug should not be given to the German wounded, but Ian made it clear that he could not agree to that.

One of the people that Ian met in Oxford was Cecil Calvert from Belfast, who was second in command to Brigadier Hugh Cairns in the neurosurgical unit there. In fact Calvert was largely in charge of the unit during Cairns' frequent absences, and gained the experience that was to prove invaluable on returning home. Florey worked closely with Cairns, whose neurosurgical unit was then situated in St Hugh's College, and this relationship proved to be fortunate since penicillin was much more effective in the infections seen in head-injured patients than in those with abdominal wounds.

The research team was to consist of a surgeon (Ian) as director, who was considered mature enough to assess the surgical infection results with and without penicillin, but still fit enough to keep up with the forward troops and wade ashore if necessary. However, Ian never considered himself as a scientific research worker, and he was accompanied by Major (later Professor) 'Scott' Thompson, a bacteriologist who identified the organisms and made the laboratory assessment. The trial was under the overall control of the Medical Research Council, but it was always to be a field trial and not a controlled study in the modern sense. Since all patients received the drug when it was available, there was no control or placebo group and it was certainly not double-blind. The team had a kind of floating status and was given a letter that entitled it to attach itself to any unit in the field that it wished; from this unit it could draw rations etc., and perhaps a stretcher to sleep on. However, they had to carry round their supplies of penicillin, as well as Scott Thompson's laboratory equipment.

ON BOARD THE *NEWFOUNDLAND*

On 2 May 1943 Ian and Major Scott Thompson said farewell to Eleanor and to Cecil and Eileen Calvert before their long journey to North Africa. As on his previous sea journey, Ian kept a detailed diary, though only for two weeks. They travelled by train to Avonmouth on the Severn and thence set off by boat on 3 May northwards round Ireland and then south to Gibraltar and Algiers. The ship was the *Newfoundland*, a hospital ship that had just brought back to London another RVH colleague, Dr Ted Lewis, who had been taken prisoner at El Alamein and released from an Italian prisoner of war camp. The ship was now going to pick up wounded from the North African campaign and return them home. It was later to be bombed and sunk at Salerno, with loss of all the doctors and many nurses, as indeed were many of the hospital ships on both sides.

There was less worry about submarines in the Atlantic than on Ian's voyage two years previously because the U-boats had nearly all been destroyed or confined to port. The *Newfoundland* was part of a convoy and had a protective escort, largely for a small ship with a red flag that was carrying nothing but ammunition and high explosives. There was still some danger of mines or air attack and they saw a few German bombers, but in the event reached Gibraltar safely. It was almost a holiday for all on board, though the nurses and doctors had to prepare to receive wounded at Algiers. There was time for a full day of celebration of matron's birthday on 8 May and Ian had time to read several books, including *Just So Stories*, which he notes that he intends to bring back for Mary Alice. He also had time to have a lot of chat with Bishop Guard, a padre who had been a prisoner of the Italians for 17 months and whom Ian describes as 'one of the finest men I met'. They arrived in Gibraltar on 9 May, and after refuelling left to arrive in Algiers on 12 May.

THE NORTH AFRICAN CAMPAIGN

We have seen that the British military bases in West Africa were essential to strengthen lines of communication with Egypt and to support it militarily against Italian forces. The argument for a new campaign was to take some of the pressure off Russia, which had been invaded and by 1942 was in a desperate plight. The aim was to invade Italy as soon as possible (described by Churchill as 'the soft underbelly of the Axis') to form a second front for Germany, and eventually a landing in France would have them fighting on three fronts. The British Eighth Army under General Montgomery therefore launched an attack on 23 October 1942, which resulted in the decisive victory over the German–Italian (Axis) forces at El Alamein in western Egypt. From then on the British moved steadily westwards, entering Tobruk (Libya) on 13 December, Benghazi on 20 December and Tripoli on 23 January 1943.

Meanwhile a second North African front had been launched in November 1942, with US troops landing at Casablanca (Morocco) and Oran (Algeria) and a combined US/British force landing at Algiers. They moved rapidly into eastern Algeria, but further advance was delayed by winter floods and strong German defence. By the spring the campaign from both sides was concentrated in Tunisia, with heavy fighting in the mountains of the west. The Eighth Army from Tripoli reached the Mareth line in March, joined up with the First Army in April and in early May was ready for the final offensive into the strongly defended Enfidaville. When this was captured on 13 May, the Axis forces in North Africa surrendered.

News of the campaign reached the *Newfoundland* as it headed for Algiers, and Ian comments in his diary on 9 May, 'Rather worried if we would get to North Africa in time for penicillin'. The work of the team in Algiers was disappointing. The 2,500 bedded hospital was full of longstanding cases of sepsis – abdominal and chest sinuses, bedsores, deep-seated infection of bones and joints – all the chronic infections so well known in the era before antibiotics. However, the time spent was useful and the team worked well. It had a small ward of 25 beds with a medical officer and QA nursing staff. They did a considerable amount of lecturing to other units, and Ian was amused to find that he was now supposed to be the expert on a drug that two months earlier he had never heard of. After a short time it became clear that the role of the drug was in the treatment or prevention of infection in acute trauma, rather than well-established infection surrounded by fibrosis and often with a poor blood supply.

While in Algiers Ian encountered General William Heneage Ogilvie (later KBE), who had asked Ian to join his Surgical Travelling Club before the war. He had just started a regime of treatment with sulphonamides and was apparently not too pleased to be told that penicillin was to replace it. Florey also appeared on the scene to oversee what Ian was doing. He had previously written to the doctors in Oxford, 'Send me your cases early, I cannot resurrect a corpse', and was not impressed by the cases received in Algiers. One evening in the mess, Heneage, talking about Florey, said to Ian 'This work always reminds me of that old Scottish hymn 'Can a mother's tender care cease towards the child she bear?'

At this stage they asked permission to move to Tripoli, which was a more acute hospital centre, though presumably there were few casualties coming in at that time. Certainly results were somewhat better here. While in Tripoli Ian records that he saw a building with the inscription 'AM XVIII' (*Anno* Mussolini 18th year). Mussolini's replacement of Our Lord was indeed short-lived.

The third centre in North Africa that they visited was Philippeville (Algeria); Ian left the penicillin team at a British general hospital there, as it was to be one of the hospitals prepared to receive casualties from Sicily. He then boarded the *St David*, which in peacetime had been a small overnight packet boat plying between southern Ireland and Wales. It had been converted into one of the hospital carriers. It was a much more basic vessel than a hospital ship, and had accommodation for only 223 patients. There were four other carriers for resuscitation and transport to North Africa, as well as 13 hospital ships more fully equipped for surgery and transporting the long-term injured back home.

It was on the *St David* that Ian sailed for Malta and almost immediately moved on to land in Sicily. As they looked up they saw the immense preparation for the air attack on 9 July – some 300–400 planes, each towing a glider. These were heading for open ground south of Syracuse (British troops) and above Gela for the Americans. Many men were lost as the gliders were sometimes released more than a mile from the shore, and bad weather and high winds sometimes carried them out to sea. The sky was black with planes, and Ian notes that for the first time he felt that success was inevitable. He did not know that on one of the planes was a recent house surgeon from the Royal Victoria Hospital, who was one of those that never managed to reach the shore.

LANDING IN SICILY

The first beach landing was near Cape Passero at Sugar Beach, at dawn on 10 July. Troops had to wade quite a distance from the launch to avoid fouling its propellers. Meanwhile the *St David* had moved five miles out, as was usual for a hospital ship or carrier so that it could put its lights on and, theoretically at least, would be immune from enemy attack. Casualties on the beach were initially very light and the main hazard was that the coils of barbed wire could be attached to a mine. The beach and surroundings were heavily mined, or had a mixture of real and bogus minefields all indicated by a sign with skull and crossbones. Eventually the Allies managed to discover a minor difference in the sign that distinguished the real from the false. Ian operated on many of those injured by the mines. The standard variety exploded below ground and split the feet open, producing a highly concentrated wound. A more dangerous type shot a projectile 2–3 feet into the air, which then exploded. This produced more serious injuries and often injured several soldiers at a time.

During the landing the enemy dropped flares to show up the soldiers on the open beach, while the British kept putting up a smoke screen to hide their movements. Altogether the allies landed 150,000 troops in the first three days opposed by 200,000 Italians and 30,000

Germans, the last of which were Panzers and armoured divisions. The fighting therefore soon became tough and the casualties severe.

A few hours after the first landing Ian volunteered to leave the hospital carrier and land on the Cape Passero beach to search for and collect the wounded. He was therefore able to get the penicillin into the wound at the earliest possible moment. When they were returning the sea was rough and transport back on the launches was very painful for the wounded, for with no lights and a smoke screen, the medical team had great difficulty in finding the *St David*. It sometimes took two and a half hours' searching. The wounded were mostly Canadians, British Royal Marine Commandos and Italians, since the airborne troops had landed further inland.

On board the *St David* conditions were fairly good, the lounge being converted into an operating theatre. Resuscitation facilities were exceptional, with oxygen and plasma laid on for every bed. The medical team with its army of nursing sisters worked flat out the whole time. The carrier had originally been intended for bringing casualties straight back to North Africa. In fact surgery was carried out continuously in it for up to 54 hours. During this time, with a strong surgical team, some 46 operations were performed. Ian himself operated for 48 hours, while the carrier was constantly subjected to air attacks. Ninety-six pints of plasma had been supplied but no blood. This was unfortunate, but it was long before the Vietnam campaign and the value of blood in trauma was not appreciated. Plasma had gained its reputation in the Spanish Civil War and in air raid casualties in Britain, where injuries were often from falling buildings, with shock but little external bleeding. One commando with both legs shattered did not respond to five pints of plasma and only recovered when he was given a fresh pint of Ian's blood. This undoubtedly saved his life and he made a good recovery.

Some months later (January 1944) Ian was awarded the DSO for his work during the Sicily landing. The citation describes his conduct on the beach and in the ship in detail and summarizes it as follows: 'By his gallant, fearless and devoted action, regardless of personal risk and safety, this officer, a brilliant and experienced surgeon, not only set an inspiring example of coolness under fire, but by employing a new technique for the first time in forward surgery, has established a new and most valuable wound treatment.' The citation also mentions his subsequent work on the Salerno beaches.

Some of the casualties had been retained in a local bivouac ashore and were not helped by the journey to the ship. Resuscitation failed in two cases, one of gross retroperitoneal haemorrhage, the other with a spinal injury with leaking cerebro-spinal fluid. On the other hand, a patient with a ruptured spleen and abdominal cavity filled with blood made a remarkably good recovery. They had 154 patients on the ship, only five of whom died. Three-quarters of the injuries were the result of bullet wounds, as is usual when fighting at close quarters, such as in beach landings. The other quarter were due to mortar bombs, mines and hand grenades. The site of the wounds was: head and neck 5 per cent, body and trunk 22 per cent, arms and shoulders 34 per cent and legs 39 per cent. As is inevitable, a few of our soldiers were injured by 'friendly fire'.

When Ian got the injured back to North Africa, Florey was on the docks with the anxious air of an expectant father. Heneage Ogilvie had already complained that the penicillin cases were getting extra special care. He probably felt that his sulphonamide programme had been superseded and that the benefits of penicillin were being exaggerated. However, it was not a controlled study and who can blame Ian for seeing that his patients got the best possible treatment, even if it meant giving the penicillin three hourly to keep the blood level high and was 'like filling the bath with the plug out'.

Ian returned to Sicily, landing at Catania on 27 July, by which time the south and west of the island (including Palermo) were in Allied hands. In the weeks that followed there was heavy fighting in the hills north-west of Etna but Nicosia was taken on 8 July, San Stefano on the coast on 31 July, Centuripe on 2 August and, after heavy fighting, Troina on 6 August. After this it only remained for the Axis forces to secure an orderly evacuation from the island.

The surgical team had the benefit of a disused school to provide cover for operating, while they slept on the slopes of the continuously erupting Mount Etna. This time it was also a more organized surgical scene. Ian went with Major Alastair MacLennan who was in command of the fifth mobile bacteriology laboratory, with a special interest in anaerobes. Scott Thompson had been left at the 48th General Hospital in Tripoli, where he was to study the bacteriology of the wounds when the patients arrived in North

Africa, and with him was Lieutenant-Colonel Jim Jeffrey, who would carry out the final surgical steps – such as secondary suturing, skin grafting and closure of amputation stumps. With the different casualty clearing stations in Sicily, each with an experienced surgeon and several field surgical units, Ian had no operating to do, but merely asked permission to treat suitable cases with penicillin. The casualties in this period were caused by road mines, mortar bombs and high explosives, with some sniping and machine gun wounds. There were also civilian casualties, tragically often children who had walked on mines. These would be deliberately placed in the vineyards, which at this time were full of magnificent blue grapes.

Ian's team confined its research to British casualties, which were easier to follow up. The results were very impressive with clean wounds ready for definitive surgery on arrival at the forward base hospital. At one stage 'Pon' D'Abreu (later Professor A.L. D'Abreu) wrote saying 'What the hell are you doing? We have never seen the like of this before.' He suggested that the wounds were so clean that they could all have been sewn up at once, and not left open for secondary suture ten days later, as is standard military practice. (However, the need for leaving wounds for secondary suture later has not gone away, and the lesson had to be re-learned by surgeons working in the Northern Ireland 'Troubles' of the 1970s). This was praise indeed, coming from one of the most experienced Eighth Army surgeons.

Unfortunately, since evacuation of casualties rested with the whim of Admiralty, although all cases were clearly marked to be taken to Tripoli, not all arrived there. Sometimes seriously ill soldiers with mortar injuries had the longest journey to make before reaching the team, while lesser gunshot wound cases arrived much sooner at casualty clearing stations. All in all, it is remarkable that such good results were obtained and were obvious to all without a scientific clinical trial. It was irritating to find that the Americans by now had generous supplies of penicillin while the official British trial was largely restricted to calcium penicillin supplied heavily diluted with sulphonamide powder for surface application by insufflator. The other form was the highly impure injectable penicillin that caused so much pain.

It is clear from the official history of the Army Medical Service in the Second World War that the Sicilian campaign was largely a success. Although there were heavy casualties, treatment was well organized, medical units managed to keep up with the moving front and land, sea and air evacuation of the wounded went according to plan. The main hazard, which should not have hit the army, was malaria. In fact, most of the south-east of Sicily was then rife with malarial mosquitoes and this was well known to the medical services. However, it was impossible to get the soldiers to take adequate precautions. Most units neglected protection against mosquito bites and refused to take mepacrine, which was freely available. The final report of the War Department is damning on this matter: 'Although past experience has repeatedly demonstrated the military importance of malaria, commanders apparently fail properly to appreciate this fact until after their own commands have suffered serious loss' (Crew, 1959, p 54).

Overall figures for British Eighth Army casualties during the Sicilian campaign were 1,649 killed, 7,018 wounded and 1,648 missing, in addition to smaller numbers of marine and airborne casualties (Crew, 1959, p. 77). These figures were considerably lower than expected. Total admissions due to malaria over this period were about 6,300. The official history states that it was in Sicily that a significant development in penicillin therapy occurred. In the forward areas wounds were treated by insufflations of penicillin and sulphonamide powder. Definitive surgical measures combined with penicillin treatment were undertaken at base hospitals in Tripoli and Sousse (Tunisia), three to twelve days after wounding.

Soon after they arrived in Sicily, it was noticeable that some of the Italian children were wearing neat jackets and suits made from the expensive nylon parachutes that had not been retrieved in time. For a night landing these parachutes were made of beautiful dark green nylon with an ivy pattern. It was reported that the QAs were also able to make elegant nightdresses out of the white nylon parachutes used for daylight landings, but naturally, Ian had no direct proof of this!

Ian stayed in Sicily until the island was finally captured and the last of the Germans were evacuated to the Italian mainland on 16 August. During this period quite a few Italian prisoners were taken, and most were delighted that the war for them was over. In fact some were taken on as orderlies and it was clear that they were very happy to help patients but would not take even a glass of water to a German.

CALABRIA AND SALERNO

Once Sicily had been conquered it was decided to press the attack into Italy as soon as possible. This was to be across the Straits of Messina, which are only a mile and a half wide. They could easily see the completely empty beaches on looking across, and when the British and Canadian troops and medical teams landed on 3 September they were unopposed. The town of Reggio di Calabria was empty; the fleeing inhabitants had not even bothered to close the doors of their houses. Highland Division soldiers danced down the main street with parasols and fancy dress 'borrowed' from some of the houses. It was a pleasant contrast to the Sicilian landing and very welcome. Ian picked up from the road a small round object about the size of a hen's egg. It turned out to be the ivory head, broken off at the neck, of a small figurine of Mussolini, which someone must have thrown out of an upstairs window. He brought it home as an unusual souvenir.

The Italian government surrendered on the day of the Allied landing, but German troops were strongly entrenched throughout Italy and were able to contest the Allied advance. It would have been possible for the army to proceed by road up through Italy to Naples and Rome. However, this would have been slow. The plan was therefore to land at several other places, notably at Taranto in the 'instep' of Italy, where there was little opposition, and in the Salerno area.

The Salerno landing on 9 September 1943 was the most hotly contested so far in the war. The enemy was expecting them and Salerno was to be held at all costs because it opened up the way to Rome. Although the beach landing was successful, the enemy were still in control, hiding in caves up the mountains that overlooked the beach. The Navy kept pounding with shellfire the mouths of the caves from the sea, but the enemy with their guns on wheels were able to retract deeply into the caves to reappear suddenly at any moment. In fact, the enemy were only finally cleared out when the Gurkhas with their kukris were sent up in the dark.

At Salerno Ian began by operating on the carrier. This time it was the converted *Ulster Prince*, familiar before and after the war as the cross-channel Belfast–Liverpool ferry. In this ship the bar was converted into an operating theatre and, as Ian says, 'I had known this room better when used for its original purpose' (Fraser, 1984).

It was roomier than the *St David* but, as with the other carrier, the ventilation system was inadequate for prolonged operating in the Italian heat. The ship later had a battle honour plaque and when it was being broken up Ian asked for a small memento. He was given the clock from the Captain's cabin, but comments that he hopes it kept better time when used at sea.

The carrier served the double role of emergency hospital and transport for the wounded back to base hospital in North Africa. Ian made one journey to Algiers and then flew back via Sicily for duties on the mainland.

Fighting between the Salerno beaches and the mountains behind continued fiercely for six days but finally the Germans began to retreat as the Allied forces moved up from the south and east.

When Ian landed at Salerno on 21 September he went in by plane – the first little plane to land – and found that he was the only doctor on board with seven young men in uniform without badges. It turned out that these were all Conscientious Objectors, Quakers who were going ashore to clear up the minefields. As Ian comments 'Their religion would not let them kill but it took away from them any fear of death. These were wonderful young men; I have always admired the Quakers, but never more than at that time' (Fraser, 1984).

ILLNESS AND RETURN HOME

Naples was finally entered on 1 October and the first phase of the Italian campaign was over. However, by this time Ian's Italian campaign had already ended, for he had suddenly realized that he was ill with a severe pain in his back etc. He had no idea what the problem was, but the illness turned out to be diphtheria – a very common complaint in North Africa. During a period of isolation at Salerno in a small cowherd's hut, the QA sisters gave him superb care. From there he was flown to Catania on a stretcher suspended from the roof of the plane. This was quite comfortable except for the fact that the plane, which had been used for dropping paratroops, had no doors and was bitterly cold.

On arrival at Catania the casualties were all laid out on the tarmac on their stretchers. This sounds pretty rough, but in fact they all later greatly appreciated the warm sun. At this stage Lieutenant Colonel

Max Rosenheim, who was later to be Lord Rosenheim, President of the Royal College of Physicians, came along. He was an old friend and, seeing Ian's tunic covering him, with the insignia of a lieutenant-colonel RAMC on the shoulder, gave him priority treatment. Ian then spent some weeks in Max Rosenheim's ward and was finally given a few days' recovery leave in Taormina. While there they were all told that Gracie Fields was expected to give a concert, but to their great disappointment she never arrived.

Next he moved on to Cairo for a few days in the 15th Scottish Hospital, a famous wartime centre. He was able to visit the operating theatre frequently when there, mostly to watch Mr Clifford Naunton Morgan FRCS closing colostomies. This was a frequently performed operation for most bowel wounds in the forward area, and, since it was often carried out hurriedly as a life-saving operation, closure was not easy. Naunton Morgan was an expert at this, often carrying out six or seven such procedures each day.

Ian had another friend in Cairo, Colonel Michael Boyd, a skilled vascular surgeon but quite eccentric. One day Ian asked to accompany him to buy a carpet. They went to the shop where all the rugs were laid out in front of them, and were given Turkish coffee. Boyd bought nothing and they went on to another shop, where the same thing happened. When they went to the third shop Ian asked him if he really wanted to buy a carpet. He replied 'No, but I really like the Turkish coffee.' At this stage Ian felt that he had seen enough carpets and rugs and tasted enough Turkish coffee to last him for the rest of his life. Michael subsequently became professor of surgery in Manchester, where he was still an eccentric and at one stage had a monkey living with him.

On full recovery, Ian moved into Shepheard's hotel for a week, but eventually he was ready for home and the transport officer arranged for a flight about three days later. Ian and a senior RAF officer whom he had come to know paid their bill and took a taxi to the airport. They were all herded into a small room to be briefed, but at this stage the transport officer announced 'I'm sorry but two people will not be able to travel tonight because I have been forced at the last minute to take two Russian war correspondents'. Inevitably, Ian and his friend were the two left behind. They were given a date three or four days later and returned to Cairo. When they got back to the airport, the same sequence happened, this time for two American flight sergeants – apparently experts on the working of the Flying Fortress and essential for the war effort. So back they went to Shepheard's, where fortunately a bed was still available. On the third occasion Ian spoke to the transport officer before he got to his feet and said 'Sergeant, what is tonight's excuse?' The reply was 'Well, I must take home a Naval sub-lieutenant and a stoker.' Our pair thought it was perhaps time to 'pull rank'. However, the transport officer became even more uncomfortable and explained that the two men (who looked more like boys) had done a magnificent job in the Mediterranean, and were now due to return home to receive the VC from George VI. So Ian and his friend returned to Cairo, feeling rather humbled and this time with no complaints. (This is one of the few occasions where Ian's memory led him astray. In his autobiography he describes these two as having been in charge of a midget submarine and going home to receive their VCs. In fact the midget submarine episode took place on 31 July 1945 when he'd just flown home from India.) Ian and his companion were lucky on the fourth occasion.

By the time Ian left, the amount of penicillin available was increasing rapidly. Jim Jeffery took over and saw the study to its conclusion, leaving the drug as a routine treatment for the remainder of the war.

As a postscript to this chapter, Ian received in 1988 a letter that is worth recording:

> Dear Namesake! I have been meaning to write to you for at least 40 years to re-establish that brief contact we made on the beach at Salerno in September 1943. I have followed your distinguished career from afar in the hope that coincidence would again bring us together, but it has not. So I pick up my pen, with no particular event or anniversary in mind, to write this letter.
>
> I was brought in to your Casualty Clearing Station on a stretcher with a couple of gunshot wounds in my chest from a passing Focke-Wolff 190. You looked at the label on my big toe which read '253913 Lt Ian Fraser, 2nd Battalion Scots Guards', and you said 'Since we have both got the same name, I'll take you next.'

Someone gave me a shot of Pentothal and I went out. When I came round you came to talk to me. I remember you said you came from Northern Ireland and I said I came from Inverness-shire. You sent me off on a hospital ship with the recommendation to leave the metal in. I have it in my chest to this day (alongside my pacemaker!)

Since that day I have met many Ian Frasers, but sadly never again you. Albany Herald is my closest neighbour in Scotland. The blind MP came quite a bit into my life. I used to take him fishing. The VC submarine commander and I often got each other's mail but we never met. The head of Wimpeys in Latin America strode into a dinner party in Lima where I once was and was the life and soul of it. The junior in my firm (Lazard Brothers) did not last very long. I never met the Labour MP. We are quite a club! …

I had four glorious children and I look upon the world with equanimity and gratitude. I am glad to be alive and I want to thank you for your contribution to that end. If ever you come to Somerset, do get in touch and visit.

Yours sincerely, Ian Fraser

The same Ian Fraser wrote to him again five years later, ending 'I cross another threshold in a fortnight's time and become a septuagenarian but, thinking of the fellow who operated on me in No 1 CCS in Salerno on 22nd September 1943, it gives me no fears.'

The 'VC submarine commander', corresponded with Ian in 1997–8 on the occasion of the erection of the memorial to James Magennis in Belfast. It is a small world, and it is not surprising that the paths of three Ian Frasers should have crossed in connection with this widespread war.

Chapter 6

Normandy

PREPARATIONS

Home leave when it came was all too short and Ian was posted to Yorkshire to a general hospital unit, preparing for the invasion of Normandy. In fact, he had been expecting consulting surgeon grading combined with a posting to India, but the urgent need now was to establish a front on the European mainland. The surgical team at this time consisted of a regular colonel who had been a brigadier but was demoted to this rank, as was not uncommon. Then there was Ian, and his No. 2 was a Canadian surgeon. The Sister in Charge of the theatre was a formidable lady who took a very active part in the planning. There was to be a large area for the ambulances, which often arrived at night and required great space to keep clear of the guy ropes. In addition they had to be able to discharge their patients rapidly while the driver had a short nap, and then get on the road again. There were ward tents for 1,000 or 1,500 beds and tents for 'triage', resuscitation, an operating theatre, and for the walking wounded who would be evacuated directly to England. They were later shown aerial photographs of the fields around Bayeux to help in making detailed plans, and were able to locate the water supply, the roads forward and an evacuation route to the harbour.

In the middle of the planning Ian was posted in March 1944 to Cambridge, the headquarters of Eastern Command. He was housed very comfortably on the Huntingdon Road, with Mrs Winifred Armstrong, a lady who couldn't do enough for the army. She also allowed Eleanor to come over, which was certainly very welcome, though again without the children. At the time when they stayed with Mrs Armstrong she had just heard that her son, a pilot in the RAF, was missing. It was only years later, when Ian met the ex-pilot at a party, that he heard the whole story.

> He was one of a crew of seven in a Lancaster bomber which was on a night bombing raid on Germany, and it had been brought down over northern Italy. The plane was a complete wreck, but as it happened the crew escaped almost undamaged. It was only after the initial jubilation died down that the Germans realised that there were no bodies. The airmen had been hidden away at separate safe houses. This was easy, as at that time there was no real love between the northern Italians and the Germans. It required much quick thinking, as a house-to-house search would have discovered the airmen, with the usual retribution on the Italians who had hidden them. Rapidly seven graves were dug, and seven coffins ordered from the local undertaker. Two parish priests conducted the sad cortege of the coffins and a few mourners down the main street – I suppose it was really a case of 'rentacrowd'. The heavy coffins, filled with stones, were decorated with a few flowers; a final prayer was said at the graveside, and everyone was happy – no one more so than my friend Watty who, hidden behind heavy curtains, had witnessed his own funeral. (Fraser, 1989, p. 51)

The consulting surgeon to Eastern Command was Major-General Heneage Ogilvie, who was based in the same house. At this time he was writing a book on war surgery and had asked the War Office for someone to relieve him. As Ian was unattached he was given the job of deputizing for Ogilvie – a task that involved going all over the south-east to visit the various medical establishments, including convalescent hospitals. Most of these buildings were commandeered schools whose large dormitories were suitable as wards. One elegant, well-known ladies' school, Roedean, allegedly had a bell push button over each girl's bed with the notice 'Ring if you want a mistress'. Many soldiers rang the bell without success.

The object of the visits was to assess the capacity of these hospitals if they were needed to provide additional beds for the Normandy casualties. They were all instructed that on a certain day they should be prepared to evacuate all possible patients and have a stock of 200 pints of blood. Of course they all readily agreed, but all asked the same question: 'When do you want us to do it?' This was one question to which Ian had no answer. In fact he did not know for certain that he was going to Normandy. These beds were never necessary as there were 22,000 beds in Normandy and approximately 14,000 casualties, but Montgomery was making sure that preparations were more than adequate.

Eventually Ian was recalled to Yorkshire to complete the hospital's preparations. Then came the time to travel down to Southampton by train with windows blacked out, and to camp in close concealment in a wood near there. On the trees were many loud speakers, and soldiers were free to move around provided they were always within earshot of instructions. When their number was called they made for the landing craft returning from Normandy and had to be ready to jump in at once.

D-DAY LANDING (6 JUNE 1944)

The hospital team set off a few days after the main D-Day landing and the journey on the small landing craft was uneventful. Because of the wide difference between high and low tide it was considered safer not to beach the craft, but to drop the ramp in moderately deep water, and get the troops to wade ashore. This, of course, was quite different from the situation in the Mediterranean landings, where they had landed dry. Ian, being short, found himself immersed up to mid-chest but when he complained to a tall chap next to him he got little sympathy. His neighbour simply pointed out that Ian was lucky to have less of himself above water as a target for the enemy snipers.

All were given a good box of rations to keep them going until the kitchens were working. One item that still seems highly original was a tin of self-heating soup. At the top of the tin was a small projecting cap and when this was loosened and touched with a match, the soup came to the boil in one or two minutes. The landing took place at Arromanches and they then had to make their way to the hospital site at Bayeux. The march was made more difficult as they had frequently to jump into a ditch to let tanks and armoured cars pass. These had naturally a high priority and were supplied with fuel from England by the famous Pluto (Pipe Line Under the Ocean). This had been laid more than halfway across the Channel even before the invasion and now within France was a six-inch pipe running along the roadside to supply not only land vehicles but also the essential air support.

One of the first people Ian met on landing was Arthur Porritt (later Sir Arthur Porritt PRCS). He was consulting surgeon to the 21st Army Group and had gone ashore very early. When he saw Ian he said 'What are you doing? I thought you were off to India but I'm b——- glad to have your help.' The result was that Ian had two or three exciting months that he had not expected in what appeared to be the best organized military medical exercise ever conceived.

SETTING UP BASE HOSPITAL

Once the medical team began to gather at Bayeux, the first priority was to set up outside toilets for the QAs and medical staff. They found a marvellous machine that had no military function whatever but was used by the telephone companies for making deep circular holes in the ground. This was attached to the back of a lorry and when dropped down vertically and driven by the engine of the lorry could create 20 circular holes ten feet deep in an hour or two. The next priority was to create some sort of camouflage; this was achieved by the rather crude expedient of cutting down some surrounding trees. The French baroness who owned the chateau where they were camped did not think much of the idea and complained bitterly. Apparently the English had done more harm to her property in two days than the Germans in the three years of occupation. However, this was inevitable as the area was a much valued source of good fresh farm produce which the Germans bought with their usual paper money. Only later did the French realize that the latter was valueless, whereas the new money coming with the 'liberation' was at least valid currency.

The hospital (108 General Hospital) was arranged along two roads meeting at a V junction that soon became known as Harley Street and Wimpole Street. Each hospital occupied many fields on each side of a road, but first they had to lay out the parking area for the ambulances. The casualties were delivered to a reception tent for triage and then moved to resuscitation, theatre and the wards as required. The hospital had tentage for 1,500 beds, and 1,000 of these were ready in five days. The first intake was 500 cases, which meant 'all hands to the pumps'. A senior surgeon was in charge of triage but the padres could be pulled in for note-taking and the dentists for anaesthesia. The scale of the operation is difficult to contemplate except by comparisons. Detailed planning enabled the quartermasters to provide beds, blankets, mattresses, pillows and much more for a hospital three times the size (in beds) of the new Royal Victoria in Belfast, all within five days, and take in 800 casualties on the fifth day.

Each surgeon had some liberty in organizing his own theatre to suit his ideas and team. Ian's theatre at Bayeux was H-shaped, with the crossbar given to central sterile supplies. Along one wall were about a dozen primus stoves, each with a fish kettle on the boil all the time. It was important not to have the primus stoves too close to the tent walls – at least one theatre was set on fire and lost because of this. The senior QA sister was in charge. The heat was unbearable and surgeons worked naked from the waist up with only an apron, gloves and mask, but for the nurses it must have been miserable.

After one long night Ian looked at the sister and saw that her face was a streaky black. The dye from her hair had run down all over her face. He was able to suggest quietly that she get it quickly washed before the young day nurses arrived on duty. Years later when she had become matron of an important London hospital, he was asked to come over to give out the nurses' prizes, and was able to recall the hectic wartime life of their charming white-haired Matron.

On each side of the H they had three operating tables, which were manned by one surgeon. This allowed one table for sedation or anaesthesia and preparation while the surgeon operated at one table and moved on, while dressing and plaster could be applied relatively at leisure. This close proximity meant that the surgeon could be informed about the new case before he finished the previous one. He could consider entry and exit bullet wounds and discuss patient positioning. The anaesthetist of course could similarly plan ahead, and was equally dependent on having good assistance with two or three patients anaesthetized at once. Anaesthesia was then much simpler and the intravenous thiopentone (Pentothal) was made up in a bowl in the morning for the whole day, so that the anaesthetist could fill a syringe directly from the bowl. Blood was now in unlimited supply and was replaced each day from England. Even penicillin, which had been experimental nine months earlier, was now freely available.

SURGERY IN THE FIELD

Fatigue in this situation did not result simply from hours of work. The first to faint were the orderlies and theatre nurses who spent a lot of time waiting for instructions. The anaesthetist was next but the surgeon was usually kept on his feet by his adrenalin; then at the end of a working session he might well be the most fatigued. There was no general agreement on how long a surgeon should work with safety to himself or patient. One can do a single long stand in a situation such as an earthquake but in an invasion, with casualties coming in steadily for two or three weeks, an organized shift must be arranged. Ian's policy was for eight hours operating, eight hours off, then back for eight hours and so on. In practice this could he maintained indefinitely, unlike the more hectic arrangements favoured by the less experienced younger men.

The wounded included British and German soldiers and French civilians; French troops went elsewhere. Ian became very friendly with one German, a Colonel Karl Zulch. He had been badly injured by a Canadian tank and required very many pints of blood. He was a charming, grey-haired and cultured man, and he and Ian became close friends. After the war in 1948 Colonel Zulch, by then a struggling lawyer near Bremen, wrote to Colonel Crowdy, who was serving in the Army of Occupation of the Rhine, to try to get in touch with Ian again. He wrote:

> Mr Fraser is a man I never shall forget. It was he [to] whom I owed my life after having been badly injured in the Normandy battle against Guard [sic] Armoured Division. He saved me not only by his surgical art but by the strong emanation of his personality. Indeed he is a real physician. We often speak of him in my family and I tell about him to friends of mine. The small photo of the Fraser family stands before me on my desk. Our hope is to meet our Irish friends here occasionally. Please transmit our most hearty greetings to Brigadier Fraser and Mrs Fraser when you see them or write. My health is satisfactory. Unfortunately I can't return to my old job at Hamburg because I was a soldier for 6 years and another man takes my seat who has the merit not to have heard any shot with ball – soldier's lot all over the world.

A note to Colonel Crowdy in response to a phone call about his needs and problems indicated that he would be very grateful for a little tea, sweets for the children and cooking fat, though he adds that the children 'were provided against hunger by supplies from abroad'. Contact with Ian and Eleanor was easily established and they were able to send over not only small luxuries but some outgrown clothes for his daughter. The letters of thanks from the children, Christopher and Angela, are charming and moving documents which Ian preserved carefully for the rest of his life. When Karl applied later to the German government for a pension for his back injury, he asked Ian to send a report. Christopher came over to visit the Fraser family in Belfast during the 1950s, Mark Fraser visited the Zulch family in 1964, and the families remained good friends until the colonel's death in 1974.

Ian also recalls an incident showing the other face of Germany. One evening he was leaving the ward and turned round to give the patients a farewell wave. He received a friendly response from all, particularly from the Germans. However, at nine o'clock next morning when he was going round, the same Germans that had been so friendly refused to look at him. He had no idea what had happened until the Sister told him that in the middle of the night a young German had been admitted. Ian went to look at him and found a soldier of 18–20 years of age, with blond hair and very ill indeed from blood loss. In fact Ian asked to have blood brought along at once for transfusion. When it was produced the young German opened his eyes and asked 'Is this British blood?' As soon as Ian said that it was, the German said 'I will not take it, I will die for Hitler', which he did a few hours later. After this the other German soldiers became as friendly as previously, confirming the view that the blond man had been an SS officer.

Another patient encountered by Ian in Normandy was Jack Kingan, from Groomsport. He was a lieutenant in the Irish Guards, which on 10–11 August 1944 had been ordered to attack a strongly held village at Sourdeval. Very heavy casualties were suffered, one of them being Jack, who came into the hospital with a bullet deep below his knee. Ian soon realized that he was an Ulsterman and that he knew his mother at home, so after finishing the operation he asked the Sister to bring him a piece of paper and scribbled a quick note to Mrs Kingan explaining that the young man's life was not in any danger nor was his limb. In fact, the note reached home before the official notice from the War Office. Jack died in August 2001 and even in his obituary, gratitude is expressed to the surgeon who operated on him in Normandy 57 years earlier.

Ian found the spell treating emergencies at Bayeux very stimulating, and he was the first to admit that he learnt much from both successes and omissions. The former included an English captain with a torn popliteal artery, which he repaired and supplemented by a lumbar sympathectomy. The captain was later able to play squash and was still sending Christmas cards 50 years later. One of the disasters was a Belgian major with a ruptured spleen which he thought he had managed satisfactorily, until the patient died and post-mortem revealed a small hole at the back of the stomach, all too easily missed in an abdomen full of blood. The outcome was particularly poignant as the Belgian had fought for the liberation of his country throughout the war but missed seeing it to a conclusion.

Tetanus was surprisingly rare during the Second World War, presumably because most troops had been immunized. However, Ian did encounter a case of 'chronic' tetanus in a French civilian who had a large wound in the front of his thigh from groin to knee. He would be talking at one moment and would suddenly develop a mild tetanic spasm. It was no real cause for concern, and they tried penicillin and other drugs on him without success. Finally, Ian resorted to a thorough excision of the infected wound followed by skin grafting, and the tetanus cleared up at once. Penicillin, by reducing sepsis and keeping wounds clean, has removed the conditions favouring the growth of tetanus bacilli, but surgical debridement is still essential.

LEAVING NORMANDY

Ian was to remain in Normandy for only four months before being recalled for leave and posting to India. Then the unit moved on to Brussels at the beginning of October and took over an old established hospital there. It became an important base hospital and the social life was active, but it lost the excitement of a forward hospital. When gathering up his few souvenirs of France he remembered some ten Camembert cheeses that he had bought in soon after arrival and hidden under his bed. These would have been a great luxury at home, and in the tent had the advantage that the smell always guided him to his camp bed in the dark or in the frequent all-pervading ground mist. However, when he went to retrieve them worms had eaten their way through the soft boxes and all the cheese had gone – except for the smell. He did manage to bring back a bottle of Calvados, which was also a welcome and distinctive local product. When Ian went to the RAF base to get a flight home he met a group who had the sad task of trying to supply the beleaguered men at Arnhem.

Chapter 7

India

A BRIEF LEAVE

Ian arrived home in October 1944 for an all-too-short leave. He had only two weeks to see Eleanor and to try to get to know the children, and felt that they had suffered enough disruption of reasonable family life. Their home in Wellington Park had been let since 1940 and the family had been living in Newcastle, in the Slieve Donard Hotel and elsewhere, for nearly four years. His father, Dr Robert Fraser, was now nearly 80 and Ian knew that by the time he returned from his far-off posting in India his father might well be dead. Altogether it was a particularly sad leave, and Ian admits that having said goodbye to his father, whom he loved and admired more than any other man, he could not suppress his tears. In the event Ian was able to see him after he returned, for Robert Moore Fraser lived until 1952.

It was during this period of wartime absence that Ian's stepmother wrote this poem, which seems to capture well the helplessness of any mother whose son goes off to face the unknown dangers of war.

> Sometimes when I am sore afraid
> Of gunshot fire or midnight raid,
> And feel myself a burden too
> Oh! Is there nothing I can do?
> A voice within me seems to say
> You can do something – You can pray.

When in the house I idle sit,
When others work, or sew or knit
It's hard not sometimes to rebel
For once I too did those things well
Then to myself I sternly say
Be not rebellious, try to pray.

When in the night I sleepless lie
And hear our planes go past on high
And know that someone young and free
Is risking life for such as me.
Then humbly to myself I'll say
Surely for such as these I'll pray.

And there is one across the sea
Whose life is very dear to me.
For he great sacrifices made
To give the sick and wounded aid.
For him in peril day by day
With heartfelt love I'll ever pray.

O Lord, my prayers are poor and weak
I cannot find the words I seek,
And worldly thoughts always creep in
And I am full of guilt and sin.
Lord, help me what to do and say
And teach me, teach me, how to pray.

A. J. F.

Before leaving for India the medical team had a briefing at the War Office. The Director-General of the Army Medical Services received them and, with great secrecy, checked that all doors were closed and someone was posted at each door. He then told them that the secret formula for a new pesticide had been acquired (by unspecified means) and that this would free the British troops in India and Burma from all bowel problems and malaria. It was known as 222, and was later to be called DDT. Its practical benefit was in the fact that for every British soldier in hospital with a bullet or surgical injury, there were 130 others in hospital with medical problems such as skin complaints, diarrhoea, blood diseases and malaria, and that 222 would deal with most of these problems. Certainly a soldier with diarrhoea was at a great disadvantage when fighting the Japanese. The final point stressed was that on no account must the formula get into enemy hands.

FLIGHT TO INDIA

A few days later they assembled at Poole Harbour in Dorset, and after an overnight stay were ready to take off by seaplane for India on 29 October 1944. The cabin of the Sunderland flying boat was oval and centrally placed, with uncomfortable aluminium seats round the sides – 40 seats and only about 20 passengers on this occasion. On each empty seat was a wooden barrel marked '222', and they knew that each barrel was worth as much to the war effort as any of them. Their luggage was in an untidy pile in the centre of the cabin with a small packed lunch. The plane had large windows and as they travelled only in daylight and flew low, they had an excellent view of the whole route. The pilot was called Brown and was a brother of the A.W. Brown who, with J. Alcock, was the first to fly non-stop across the Atlantic in 1919.

A flying boat cannot take off from smooth water, so they usually had to make a few journeys back and forth to produce some waves. Then on the crest of a wave they became airborne. On the first day they flew south, skirting France and Spain, and landed in the harbour at Gibraltar in time for afternoon tea. They had dinner in the hills above, entertained by the monkeys, and enjoyed the peacetime atmosphere there. The only disturbance was that the ships in the harbour kept starting their engines and propellers to deter any enemy diver who might try to attach a mine to the ship.

On the next day they took off early and spent that night on an empty island called Djerba, just off the coast of Tunisia. They had some excellent lobsters, bought a few large sponges and had a midnight bathe in the Mediterranean. This island has since become a tourist resort with packed beaches and large skyscrapers. On the third day they landed on the Nile near Cairo and Ian renewed his acquaintance with Shepheard's Hotel. Next day after a 5 a.m. start they made a small diversion via the 'Garden of Eden' before landing at Bahrain for dinner and another swim. The Garden of Eden is alleged to have been at the junction of the Tigris and Euphrates in

Iraq but, as Ian says, 'I could not see a tree that might bear a fruit that would have tempted Adam, much less myself; nor indeed, could I see a fig tree that could have given Eve any protective covering' (Fraser, 1989, p. 65). From Bahrain they flew to Karachi and, after an evening of talk and meeting people, flew by ordinary plane to Delhi. A journey that would now be covered in about six hours had taken six days, but at least they had time to get to know each other and have some good dinners in hotels.

SURGEON TO CENTRAL COMMAND

Ian's appointment was as consultant surgeon to the Central Command with the rank of colonel, rising to brigadier at the beginning of 1945. This was the large block in the centre of India between the South, North-East and North-West Commands. The area had had a consultant physician for a year but no surgeon – understandable with the ratio of medical to surgical problems – and in spite of optimism regarding 222, the ratio of medical to surgical problems did not fall below 10 to 1. The post was now created with the oncoming Burma campaign about to begin, and many casualties were expected to come back to India. The Headquarters of the Command was in Agra and Ian was comfortably placed in the Cecil Hotel.

The consultant physician was Brigadier Bernard Schlesinger, formerly a paediatrician from Great Ormond Street, who stayed in another hotel, the Lauries. They had never met before but became life-long friends. Eleanor and Ian often stayed with him subsequently in London or Newbury and got to know his son, John Schlesinger, the film producer. The main function of these senior officers was to visit regularly all the main hospitals, Indian and British, active and convalescent, as well as POW camps and hospitals for Japanese prisoners. They always visited the hospitals separately, as it was easier for the Commanding Officer of the hospital to deal with one person at a time. Bernard took with him an impressive large attaché case which was assumed at first to contain his medical equipment, though word soon got around that it was for squash racket, shirts, shorts and shoes. It was also rumoured that if a hospital could give him a good game of squash it got a high rating for efficiency.

Ian used to cycle daily to his office in the Agra Cantonments. This was, of course, cheaper than a car and not necessarily slower. However, the real pleasure was to be able to cycle after dinner the two miles to gaze at the Taj Mahal with the moon coming up behind it, and to hear the frogs croaking. Ian did this often, and it was some consolation for the loneliness of being so far from the family in Belfast.

His nine months in India were largely administrative, with some lecturing and hospital inspections, balanced by seeing patients and operating whenever time was available. In the earlier weeks he visited the nearer towns of Lucknow and Cawnpore and in December paid a ten-day visit by train to the Lahore area. From Lahore he was driven round the towns and camps of Ferozepore, Pathankot, Sialkot, and Julundur, scattered on either side of the present Pakistan–India border. In these places, as well as looking round the wards and operating theatres, Ian gave his well-rehearsed lectures on penicillin or others on forward surgery, wound management, etc.

He had hardly returned to Agra before he was off again to a conference in Delhi and then by train (with several changes) to Bikaner in western Rajastan. There the maharaja had generously provided hospitals for British, Indian and Japanese troops. The Japanese wounded were often very ill, having tried to commit suicide rather than be taken prisoner. On his first visit Ian was accommodated in an elegant guesthouse hotel, but on one of his later visits he was invited to stay in the palace itself. Both were certainly better than the tent attached to a hospital where he was often put up elsewhere. The December visit began with a garden party, reception, dinner and dance, all very enjoyable but hardly a preparation for two days of hospital visits and a clinical conference.

Christmas was uneventful and he then returned to Lahore, this time by air, for the conference of All-India Surgeons. This visit gave him a chance for a quick trip to Amritsar to see the Golden Temple and to be reminded of the notorious massacre at Jallianwalla Bagh, where British troops in 1919 had fired on a crowd who had broken the martial law restrictions. Later in January it was south to Ajmer and Mhow, and in the following week to Benares in the far west of the Command. This city was a complete cultural shock for its overcrowding, poverty and yet central role for Hindus as a place of cremation on the banks of the Ganges. Ideally the bodies were burned on a wooden pyre and the ashes strewn on the river, but lack of dry wood often meant that a considerable amount of charred remains were pushed in. This, combined with the practice of ritual bathing in the river, made the city both fascinating and distasteful to westerners.

In general Ian travelled by train in India; one of the souvenirs he brought home was a detailed map of its complex rail network. India under British rule developed this excellent system, which was ideal for covering the long distances over difficult terrain and was helped by India's plentiful coal supplies. The only problem was that many of the journeys were overnight, though fortunately Ian was still young enough to get some sleep on such trains. For the longer journeys he sometimes travelled by air, but this was risky on the small planes that they used. His diary for 17 February when he was returning from Jubbulpore in the Central Provinces reads 'Plane smashed. Got away with a few bruises!' On the roads he had, of course, a driver, but the cars frequently broke down and the driver had also to be a mechanic.

In India Ian saw two cases that were certainly new to him – cases of true hyperthermia. This was in two marines who got on the train at Bombay to go north and were too drunk to realize that the fan in the carriage was not working. The normal practice in the circumstances was to have a zinc water container on the floor of the carriage, into which one could stick one's feet. The foot bath could be kept cold with ice supplied at the many stations on the way. Unfortunately the men were incapable of making sensible decisions and became hotter and hotter until by the time they reached Agra, their temperature had reached well over 105°F. They suffered irreversible brain damage and after a few days in hospital had to be invalided home.

In April 1945 his visit to Bikaner coincided with a visit from Lord and Lady Mountbatten and they all had an elegant dinner including much food covered with aspic. At six o'clock on the next morning Lady Edwina was due to inspect the four units with Ian in attendance. When the time came only he and she were able to be present as all her entourage were stricken with food poisoning. Aspic was certainly to blame, for in hot climates it is an ideal culture medium for growing organisms of all kinds. Lady Mountbatten was a tough lady and took her duties seriously, for she always had an appropriate word for the Gurkha, Pathan or Madrasi soldiers in their own language.

One of the minor irritations was the loss of his only souvenir of the early days of penicillin. He had a little glass bottle of penicillin that he kept for showing to the audience when he gave an occasional lecture on the drug, not yet available in India. One night when going to bed he left it on his dressing table near the open window. In the morning it was gone. He asked his bearer about it but he could only attribute the disappearance to an inquisitive monkey that had taken a fancy to the bottle with its shiny top.

Ian came across many old friends from Queen's when in India. He recalled coming upon Lieutenant-Colonel John S. Logan near Nagpur when John's car had broken down, and fortunately was able to offer him a lift back to hospital.

Communication with Britain continued throughout Ian's stay, and by 1945 he was thinking more and more of his return to civilian life. In March he was congratulating Sir Alfred Webb-Johnston of the Royal College of Surgeons on his baronetcy and subscribing to the college's rebuilding fund after severe damage in the air raids on London. His administrative duties included writing recommendations for postings in India and appointments for his officers when they achieved their hoped-for demobilization. He planned for his own return by ordering books from Lewis's of London, to be sent to Newcastle. He also managed to maintain contact with the Order of St John, secured the admission of his RAMC colleague Major-General Sir Ernest Cowell to the Order and set the wheels in motion for the admission of the Maharaja of Bikaner.

RELAXATION IN INDIA

Fortunately for Ian, the province of Kashmir was included in the Central Command. He had no official duties there but did manage to get a holiday break in the area in June 1945. As always in India he went with his Indian bearer and had the choice of staying in a houseboat on the lake at Shrinagar or in a hotel. In the event he chose the hotel because it was notorious that all the vegetables were washed in the same lake water into which the boat's effluent was discharged. The hotel also, of course, gave him much more flexibility for shopping and sightseeing. For shopping he bought the inevitable sari material, which Eleanor turned into a gorgeous evening dress when it was brought home. Less appreciated was a fur coat, which caused him much worry. He had heard that such things packed in sacking were often eaten by rats when lying on the quay at Bombay. The shopkeeper, of course, denied this but offered to pack it in a secure tin box for a special price. He even showed it to Ian all packed up when he went to pay on the next day. In due course the coat arrived at home wrapped in sacking without any box. Fortunately it wasn't eaten, but Eleanor, having worn it once so as not to hurt his feelings, soon passed it on to another relative. He did manage to bring home some lovely handmade rugs, pashmina shawls and table mats, which were much more successful.

When in Kashmir Ian made the usual visit to Gulmarg in the foothills of the Himalayas, on horseback. He had never claimed to be a horseman and felt very unsafe as the horse skilfully picked its way along the edge of terrifying cliffs. The horses have since been replaced by 'clapped out' taxis, but the journey remained equally unsafe 30 years later.

NEARING INDEPENDENCE AND THE END OF THE WAR

Towards the end of his tour of India Ian noticed a distinct change in attitudes. Slogans such as 'British get out' began to appear on the walls and, while relationships among his own staff were unchanged, things were different in public. He regularly used the midnight sleeper train from Delhi and usually if there was no sleeper, some young officer would be prepared to give up his berth to the RAMC brigadier. Suddenly this all changed. The young Indian officers were apparently sound asleep and the brigadier would have to sleep on the floor.

The holiday in Kashmir, which should have been for four weeks, was reduced to two by plans to return home and he had a frantic rush in early July, boxing up his general belongings and new purchases. He had clinical and administrative work to complete and yet he wanted to get home to be with the family in Newcastle for the summer months. The university and hospital were also anxious to have as many as possible of the experienced teaching staff back for the beginning of the academic year.

In the end things happened quickly. He sold his bicycle to his bearer for £2 and packed up. He heard later that Bernard Schlesinger had given his car to his bearer as a present, but satisfied himself with the thought that the car was worth no more than the bicycle. Finally he managed to get a sleeper from Delhi to Bombay and a flight home from Bombay on 20 July.

The flight home was rapid and easy with only a quick stop for refuelling at Bahrain. Next stop was the Victoria Barracks in Belfast to get his demob suit, shirt, socks, shoes, etc. Like many another, the suit was worn till it became too shabby to be seen in public. By September he was back at work in his old hospitals.

'A GOOD WAR'

Ian had what was often described by soldiers as 'a good war'. The phrase is rather jarring in these anti-militaristic times, but we can easily see what was meant when we reckon what he gained and what he might have suffered. Of course he was fortunate in escaping death or serious injury. At least 30 Queen's doctors were killed during Second World War, many of whom had recently passed through the Royal Victoria Hospital. He was also fortunate in escaping capture and prolonged imprisonment, as was the fate of Dr Ted Lewis, Dr Sinclair Irwin, Dr Tom Smiley and Dr Frank Pantridge.

It was really chance that determined where one was sent initially in the war, and the Gold Coast, although not very exciting, was certainly preferable to France and the horrors of Dunkirk. Ian saw that he could contribute more outside West Africa in 1943 and was exceptionally lucky in being assigned to the penicillin trial. In the event he was the right man for the job – enterprising, tactful and a good organizer – and it made his reputation. Because of illness he escaped the miseries of the 1943/4 winter in Italy, and returned home. Again, good luck resulted in his short and busy posting to France, which gave him experience of real front-line surgery and a chance to increase further his contacts with the British medical establishment. He gained experience there in the management of trauma, which is never wasted and is still applicable in dealing with victims of the motor car and civil disturbance. In the Gold Coast and India he greatly increased his knowledge of tropical medicine while keeping up some practical experience of civilian surgery in men, women and children. Equally valuable was his skill in managing people, which was put to the test in his successive postings in Africa, Italy, France and India. 'Management' was not a term much used in early post-war medicine, but the skills were necessary in hospitals, university, royal colleges and the Order of St John.

Finally, there was the award of the DSO for his courage and skill in Sicily and Italy. This award is second in distinction only to the Victoria Cross and would always be directly or subconsciously considered in his further progress up the ladder. In all, Ian ended the war with seven medals, as well as other non-military decorations. He could have remained quietly in West Africa, gaining promotion steadily, but he chose much more exciting, risky and, in the end, rewarding fields and this aspect cannot all be put down to good luck. He was not unique but he did have a very varied medical experience, which he brought back to his hospital and the wider world.

Chapter 8

Return from the war

THE CHILDREN'S HOSPITAL

Ian was demobilized in September1945 and like most ex-servicemen, found his old post waiting for him. The work in the Children's Hospital had been carried on during the war by Professor P.T. Crymble and Mr James Loughridge. When Ian returned he was immediately appointed honorary attending surgeon to replace P.T. Crymble, who was due to retire at the age of 65. Ian's practical problem was that over the previous five years he had operated on very few children, and he admitted that he had to struggle to regain his old skills in paediatric surgery. In particular a waiting list had built up for repair of the complicated penile deformity, hypospadias. Fortunately he was able to persuade Mr Denis Browne of Great Ormond Street, a real expert in the field, to come over and the waiting list of 17 cases was cleared up in three strenuous days. The operating sessions were attended by a succession of surgical registrars from all over Northern Ireland so that there was a considerable educational benefit from the exercise. Denis refused to take a fee but was rewarded by some pleasant social dinners and a supply of the best of local produce – a ham, a turkey and several lobsters.

Naturally, Ian did pick up the threads of work in the Children's Hospital and, in fact, he continued to work there until his retirement in 1966. He recognized in many of his writings that although he practised adult and paediatric surgery, the latter ought to be regarded as a separate discipline. He could see that the complexities of conditions such as Hirschsprung's disease (of the colon), hare lip and cleft palate required expert and specialized skills, but he enjoyed carrying out a wide range of surgery and meeting a diverse range of people. He describes how he kept some of his child patients, such as achondroplasiacs (dwarfs) coming back to his clinics both for teaching purposes and because they had become 'friends'.

The other factor delaying specialization throughout medicine was economics. The surgeon wanted a large private practice and could not afford to confine himself, for instance, to paediatric or prostate surgery, even in his public hospital work, since skills in all fields had to be maintained.

The 1950s were a difficult period for surgery in the Children's Hospital. A succession of surgical registrars worked there, gaining experience but without expert training in its paediatric aspects. In all fields of medicine there was a shortage of consultant posts and no one wanted to specialize without some hope of a post in Northern Ireland. Ian Fraser was Chairman of the Medical Staff Committee of the hospital 1954–7 and he, along with Norman Hughes (plastic surgery) and James Loughridge, encouraged Brian Smith to go away to Great Ormond Street, London, and to Liverpool to obtain the necessary specialized training. As a result Brian Smith was appointed as the first paediatric surgeon in the province in 1959. It was on Ian's recommendation to Lord Glentoran that the matron, Miss Molly Hudson, was awarded an OBE in 1954.

In his later years on the staff of the hospital Ian did virtually no clinical work and always had good paediatric surgical registrars who were very happy to carry on with his operating sessions and clinics. In fact, he was largely a figurehead coming in for the main social occasions of the hospital, for, like most small hospitals, it was very closely bound together by loyalty and comradeship. Much of this involvement continued long after his retirement, and Ian was just the right man to speak at the funeral of Molly Hudson in 1984. She had come from Lancashire in 1948 at the time when the Health Service was starting, and had remained as matron for 36 years. Before that, as we have seen, the hospital ran as in the nineteenth century, with nurses doing everything from floor-cleaning to laying out the dead and matron doing everything from ordering stores to giving anaesthetics. Her time saw the expansion of the nursing staff from 33 to 187 and specialization in every field of paediatrics. However, most of all Ian pays tribute to her human and humane qualities. He remembers on Christmas Eve 1982 finding her and her

Dr Robert Moore Fraser (1865-1952)

Dr Alexander Cuthbert (1834-1876)

RBAI Under-XV Rugby Team 1915-6, with Ian Fraser on the left of the seated row

Resident medical staff, Royal Victoria Hospital, 1923-4
(left to right, standing) J.W. Heney, W.C. Henry, H.H. Stewart, J.R. Wheeler,
J.A.L. Johnston, C.H. Kerr, I. Fraser and J.M. Cole (Dispenser)
(seated) E. Armstrong, O.M. Ferguson, W.A. Brown, Col. C.V. Forrest (Superintendent),
C. Turner, H.M. Koeller and J.A. Smyth

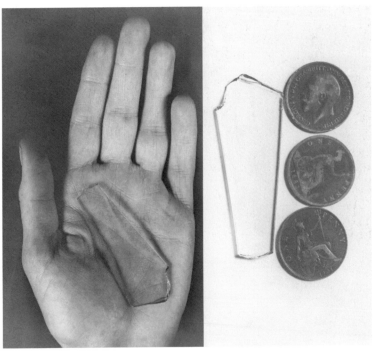

*Piece of glass removed from a millworker's hand which had been there
unsuspected for many months (1933)*

Brigadier Ian Fraser, Mark, Mary Alice and Eleanor 1945

Party at Royal Victoria Hospital to celebrate Ian's receiving a knighthood 1963, with Dr Robert Marshall, Miss Florence Elliott, Eleanor and Ian, also Sir John Biggart in white coat behind

Armorial bookplate 1969

Award of Honorary MRCPI 1977
(left to right) Prof C.H.G. Macafee, Sir Ian Fraser, Dr Alan Grant (President RCPI)
and Mr Jack Lynch (Taoiseach)

Award of Honorary FRCSI to Loyal Davis 1981 (Loyal Davis, James O'Connell PRCSI,
Sir Ian Fraser, Nancy Reagan, Ronald Reagan and Sean Donlon)

Family group 1982, with Mark Fraser, Eleanor Fraser, Una Davidson, Mary Alice Trustram Eve and Sir Ian Fraser

Unveiling of memorial plaque in Ward 18 in 1992 in honour of the Working Men's Committee (Sir Ian Fraser, Mr Aires Barros d'Sa, Miss Florence Elliott (ex-matron), Sister Janet Robson, Mr John Hood and Sister Judith McClements)

Award of Honorary LLD from QUB 1992 (Sir Gordon Beveridge, Clare Macmahon and Sir Ian Fraser)

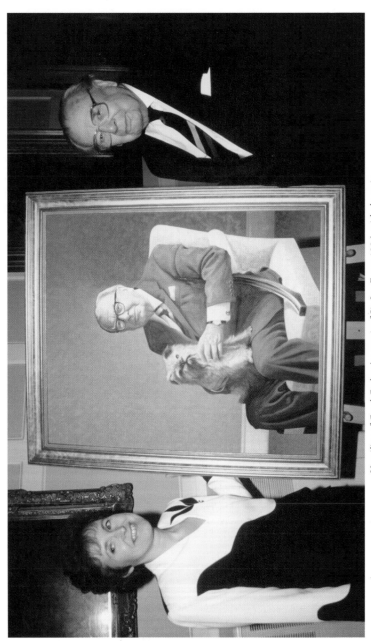

Unveiling of Carol Graham's portrait of Sir Ian Fraser 1994, with the artist

household in tears at the death of her beloved dog, killed near her home by a car. The next day he called with some trepidation to cheer her up, but found her back to her old self again; on her lap was a minute black object that turned out to be a poodle pup. It had been left in that morning by an old friend and surgical colleague, Jimmy Piggott, and never was a gift more appreciated.

THE ROYAL VICTORIA HOSPITAL

Having arrived back at the Royal Victoria Hospital in October 1945, Ian, as well as James Loughridge and Eric McMechan, was given assistant surgeon status. Ian McClure and T.H. Crozier were appointed as assistant gynaecologist and assistant physician respectively. All of them appear to have been immediately appointed to the Medical Staff Committee, which at that time numbered about 30, and in November Ian was appointed lecturer in surgery to the nurses. Thereafter he settled down to the routine duties of surgeon, teacher and committee man within the hospital and to a growing private practice outside it.

The advent of the National Health Service in July 1948 brought a major change to all hospital doctors. All honorary physicians and surgeons, whether with assistant or attending status, were described as 'consultants'. Furthermore, all were now paid a salary in respect of their sessional commitment to the NHS, still having the right to private practice. The NHS, was not, of course, introduced for the benefit of doctors but because it was no longer possible to fund hospitals from charitable or municipal funds. The vast majority of hospitals now came under central control – in Northern Ireland under the Hospitals Authority – and this slowly enabled them to improve buildings, staffing of all kinds, and equipment.

When Ian was designated consultant in 1948 he was one of several in this position, as described above, but he was the most senior in terms of age and date and number of qualifications. His ex-service status also gave him an advantage, and the death of Cecil Calvert in April 1956 left him as the senior surgeon in the hospital.

The next landmark in Ian's career at the Royal Victoria Hospital was his nomination to give the Annual Oration to students at the start of the winter academic session in 1952. These annual lectures had continued intermittently from 1827 and with few gaps during the twentieth century. The orator was almost invariably chosen in the order of appointment to the medical staff, and with the small staff of that period every member of staff could become the orator. Ian chose as his title 'The heritage of the Royal Victoria Hospital' and managed to give not only the familiar history of the first 155 years of the hospital's existence, but an appraisal of medical developments over the period. He reminds us that love of humanity means love of the art and practice of medicine, and that science without sense is valueless. It remains, after 50 years, a good basis for medical practice.

The role of chairman of medical staff, like that of orator, came round in order of seniority but, since the term of office was normally for two years, many members of staff died or retired before becoming chairman (for example Mr Barney Purce). In the event, Ian's time as chairman came round for the years 1960–1. It is not certain why he remained as chairman for only one year, but it is most likely that he felt that having served from May 1960 to May 1961, a second year would clash with his role as president elect of the BMA (Chapter 9). The annual meeting of the BMA was planned for Belfast in July 1962, and it probably seemed unwise to be chairman of medical staff throughout the preparatory year.

Ian maintained his surgical work at the Royal Victoria Hospital, as far as his duties allowed, until his retirement in 1966. He was a fast and dextrous surgeon but inevitably his roles as committee member, chairman or president of so many bodies took him away from the work he loved. On the other hand his greatest contribution to the hospital, province and beyond was probably as their public representative. He had the charm and charisma, as well as the expert knowledge, to make a real contribution to his various committees.

His retirement was by no means the end of his connection with the Royal Victoria Hospital. He was a regular attender at staff dinners, missing only in the last year of his life. The old surgical extern theatre – intimate but very uncomfortable – was named the Sir Ian Fraser theatre in 1982. His last clinical case presentation at a surgeon's meeting was on 10 April 1992 when, along with Norman Nevin and Denis Gough, he presented a case of myositis ossificans progressiva. What was truly remarkable was that Ian had first seen the patient in 1931 at the age of two and had talked to his parents about likely problems. The patient subsequently became more and more disabled but with supportive parents, his own positive approach to life and good state care, did manage to have a worthwhile life. Ian also came back formally in 1992, along with the ex-matron, Florence Elliott, to unveil a plaque to the Working Men's Committee in Ward 18.

THE CHAIR OF SURGERY

Professor Crymble retired from the chair of surgery in 1947 having already retired from his post at the Children's Hospital, and the chair was advertised in the usual way. Until this time nearly all chairs had been filled by Irishmen, and the expectation was that it would go to one of the brightest of Queen's University graduates, Ian Fraser. However, it had been decided within the Faculty of Medicine that chairs would in future involve a research commitment and to facilitate this the professor would have to withdraw from private practice, in return for which his salary would be increased to £1,500. Ian, as one would expect, applied for the chair and would certainly have been appointed if he had been prepared to accept the new conditions. However, he declined, probably because he was not really trained for academic research, disliked experimentation on animals and also was reluctant to give up his hard-won private practice, which he really enjoyed. It is likely that he felt bitter in having to abandon a long cherished ambition, but the university clearly felt the need to change the direction of academic medicine regardless of personalities.

Later, in his David Torrens Lecture of 1979, Ian was to describe the creation of the full-time chair in surgery as one of the milestones of progress in surgical training. He saw that it helped to break down barriers of the old system where junior surgeons had been 'apprenticed' to a single surgeon, in Ian's case Andrew Fullerton. In the era following the Second World War the trainee could rotate round most of the surgical specialities, gaining experience in all fields, including animal research, and supervised broadly by the Professor of Surgery. It was a far cry from Ian's training of assisting at his chief's operations, giving his lectures when required and opening the classroom and car doors for the great man.

In retrospect it is clear that Ian made the right decision. The University subsequently invited Harold Rodgers from St Bartholomew's Hospital in London, who also had an excellent record in the RAMC, to apply and appointed him in October 1947. Rodgers was six years younger than Ian and, probably because he was an 'outsider', was able to create a new type of department, with laboratory, animal house and surgical research fellows. It was essential for Queen's to move in this direction and it applied the same formula to medicine in 1950 to replace Professor W.W.D. Thomson, bringing in Graham Bull from South Africa and Hammersmith with a well-established research record.

RVH ALPHABETS

The tradition of writing satirical alphabets about the hospital dates back to the 1890s, with a second one in 1930 and a third in 1960. They were distributed anonymously, presumably to allow the authors freedom to criticize their colleagues, but the authors were usually known as R.J. Johnstone, Hugh Calwell (1930) and Ian Fraser (1960). All three alphabets were published in the *Ulster Medical Journal* in 1993, with some explanatory notes, though there are many references in the 1890s alphabet whose meaning is now lost. In 1930 Hugh Calwell characterizes Ian, while a registrar with Andrew Fullerton, as follows:

> F is for Fraser who keeps Andy right:
> He ne'er at the cherry takes more than one bite.

They were very familiar to Ian and are frequently quoted in his writings. When his time came to write his own alphabet he highlighted a new set of names and managed a dig at the surgeon 'spreading the dung', the professor 'occasionally here' and the neurologist with 'hardly a moment to tap scraggy knees'. The Fraser alphabet runs as follows:

A's the Aorta that all must rely on:
if Reggie's in doubt he slips in some nylon.

B is for Brown with his rag and his bottle:
I am told that at Stormont there are some he would throttle.

C is for Craig – not tall or good looking:
golf not too bad but a habit of hooking.

D is for Desmond of blood sugar fame:
I am told with his books he has made a great name.

E is for Ernest, bald and sunburned:
his motto is always 'leave no stone unturned'.

F is for Frankie, I mean Frankie P.,
who knows all the heart waves from P through to T.

G is George Johnston, a surgeon with skill:
the 'gun' now has made his mortality – nil.

H is for Harley – his skill with the pill
keeps pregnancies down to virtually nil.

I is for Irwin, a strong silent man
who for vascular disease does the best that he can.

J is Jack Pinkerton – a midwife No. 1:
occasionally here when not chasing the sun.

K is for Kennedy – this time it is Joe:
if you can't pass your water he'll soon make it flow.

L is for Logan for years nicknamed Bunny:
his political views are serious – not funny.

M is for McKeown – the lady professor:
a friend to us all, her students all bless her.

N is for Nevin professor genetic
who says it's our genes that make us phrenetic.

O is for Osterberg, expert with bones:
a true successor to Sir Robert Jones.

P is for Froggatt – his first name is Peter:
the dean for three years – his hair could be neater.

Q's are the queer ones – I mean mental – not sex:
they're odd in their ways – yet morals not lax.

R is for Douglas – the Scottish Rob Roy:
up to date he has proven he's the 'broth of a boy'.

S is for Swallow, whose tapping of keys
leaves hardly a moment to tap scraggy knees.

T is Tom Smiley – he'll chop out a lung,
if he's not on his farm busy spreading the dung.

U's the Unknown who writes all this drivel
and signs it 'anon' fearing action for libel.

V is the Vagus, poor innocent nerve
Which Terence attacks with his usual verve.

W is Willoughby the Methody chap:
I hear the colons fall into his lap.

X are the X-rays now taken with care:
there'll be no overdosage if our Teddy is there.

Y's are the Young men who daily report
that they do the work when their chiefs are at court.

Z is the plasty that Norman produces:
a knife and some forceps are all that he uses.

TEACHING AND BEDSIDE MANNER

Ian's abilities as a teacher were apparent from the 1930s. His tutorials or 'grinds' were popular and successful, which probably led to his being elected president of the BMSA in 1939. During the war one of his important roles in the Gold Coast, North Africa and India was lecturing and conducting tutorials. During the post-war period his ward rounds were particularly popular, since he always had some appropriate story or demonstration to fix salient features in the student's memory. His popularity as a teacher is admirably captured in an anonymous article in *Snakes Alive*, the BMSA magazine, of *c*.1960.

> In the stygian gloom which often passes for a medical curriculum, an occasional light shines. This light is crescent-shaped, Cheshire cat wise and is a grin, and the grin is the ineluctable essence of the character; above the grin are eyes, piercing in their serious mien, and yet always seeming to twinkle … On any Tuesday or Friday morning … you can locate him by finding the ward kitchen filled with students trying to fight their way into the ward … He marches to the foot of the bed, acolytes trotting behind with drawing pad, and seizes the foot of the patient; with a shake of the foot and a thump on the chest, the subject is convinced by some alchemy that all is well with the world, that he himself is the prize patient, and that everyone is delighted and pleased with the splendid recovery he is making. He turns to the class. Seizes the block. Out with the golden pencil, preferably someone else's. 'Well now, this patient had such and such. And the operation is? Yes that's it. And we did it this way. Of course in some provincial centres, like London, they do other things, but I always do it this way.'

One memorable occasion was when he was talking about breast surgery in the middle of the ward and asked the assembled students the innocent question 'Do you know how to bandage a breast?' Naturally no one knew – or would admit to knowing. So he calls out one large young man, saying 'Sister, some gamgee please' and when this comes, the youth (minus white coat and jacket) is suitably fitted with two 'breasts'. Sister was then asked to demonstrate the bandaging procedure to the great delight of students, nurses and, probably most of all, the female patients.

Of course the sequel to the story is when he tried to demonstrate in the course of the ward round some point of surface anatomy on one of the girl students. Warning of this procedure had usually gone round and, if the girl couldn't escape to the back of the class, she managed to keep her arms firmly folded across her chest until the demonstration was over, leaving the long-suffering sister to act as model.

While he might occasionally make fun of medical students, Ian was invariably charming to all his patients. This was in contrast to some of his colleagues who could be quite unfeeling, subjecting them to some exhausting examination or sarcastic remarks if the patient did not appear to understand what was going on. There is the well-known story of Dr T.H. Crozier, when he was examining a patient's ears. The patient asked him 'Doctor, can you see my brains?' To which T.H.C. replied 'Madam, this is an auriscope, not a microscope.'

Ian's approach was completely different. One day he came into a follow-up clinic in the Children's Hospital and little Johnny and his mother were brought in for review of an appendectomy on the boy six weeks previously. A quick glance at the notes told him the story, though he had never seen the patient before. In a few words he made the mother aware that 'we' had operated just in time to prevent peritonitis. Not a word was said that wasn't true, and Johnny and his mother were made to feel important and fortunate that they had come to such a good hospital and been seen by such a great surgeon.

Of course the charm did not always work. There was one memorable occasion on a ward round when Ian approached a lady of the locality and said 'You're looking much better than when I saw you last, my dear.' To which she replied firmly 'Mr Fraser, a' never seen ye before in my life.'

THE BLEEDING BOWL SAGA

Ian collected antiques all his married life, but one of his favourite fields, on account of their surgical interest, was bleeding bowls. Over the years he built up a collection of some thirty delph bowls. Gradually he became a considerable authority in the field and was undoubtedly very fond of them. Then suddenly, in a surprising and dramatic gesture, he gave nearly all of them away. On 7 November 1981, just before his 80th birthday, he invited some 50 of his friends, family and junior colleagues (with wives) to a dinner in the Royal Victoria Hospital, arranged by his colleague Ernie Morrison. After dinner everyone was invited to go into another room where about 30 bowls were on display, each labelled with the name of one of the surgeons. It seems that, like many collectors, he felt uncertain as to what should be the fate of the collection as he became older. He therefore with typical generosity chose a method of disposal of the bleeding bowls to find 'a good home' for them and to give his friends something to remember him by.

It should be said that Ian's generosity to his registrars was well known. Anyone who went to assist him with a private case always received a present – usually a £10 note in the days when a house surgeon's annual salary was only £75 (Love, 1998). Harold Love also records that when Bill Cochran, still a surgical senior registrar in the Children's Hospital, was seriously ill, Ian turned up at his back door bearing wine and a hamper of food. This was a far cry from the extrovert, confident surgeon, a master of the throwaway line and the quick riposte. However he considered it only right that he should recognize the help of his junior colleagues generously, since they frequently assisted with or finished difficult cases and made possible his widespread surgically related activities.

FAMILY LIFE

Return from the war of any soldier notoriously requires a lot of readjustment on all sides, but fortunately the omens here were all favourable. Ian and Eleanor had managed some time together during his occasional periods of leave, though Ian had missed the pleasure of seeing the children as babies and toddlers. When he returned in late 1945 Mary Alice was 7 and Mark was 6. However, he was back for the more difficult period of their growing up, even if a successful doctor always seems to be an absentee parent. Indeed, Ian's career took him away at least as much as the much-criticized 'absentee professor', and for the remaining 20 years of his working life he was constantly away in Dublin, London or elsewhere in the United Kingdom at least once a month. Medical conferences came round several times a year and if Eleanor was able to get to many of these, the children certainly did not. Una Davidson was there to provide care and stability until the children went to boarding school in the 1950s. After this she moved out to a flat of her own off the Malone Road, but still came up daily to provide help and companionship for Eleanor, and frequently cooked for them. This continued right up to Eleanor's death in 1992.

The family returned to live in 33 Wellington Park in 1945 and continued to live there until 1951. By this time they needed more space both indoors and outside – rooms of their own and room to be creative and noisy, so they moved to the larger and more modern

19 Upper Malone Road with a well laid out half acre of garden. Mary Alice went first to Richmond Lodge School, which subsequently amalgamated with Ashley House School. The decision had been made that both would go to boarding schools in England, and Mary Alice went to Downe House in Berkshire 1949–1955. She then spent a year at the Eastbourne School of Domestic Economy (which had the doubtful distinction of having Dr John Bodkin Adams as its attendant doctor) and then on to France and London for more sophisticated cordon bleu training. On 15 December 1962 in St Bride's, Fleet Street, London, Mary Alice married John Roy Trustram Eve and they settled in the south of England.

Mark had the early part of his schooling at Brackenber House, before boarding at Haileybury College, Herts, 1953–9, and went on to study medicine at Clare College, Cambridge and the Middlesex Hospital, London. He graduated MA MB BChir in 1965 and then faced the difficult decision as to whether to follow the surgical path of his father or the general practice path of his grandfather. He took the FRCSI exams in 1971, the DA Eng in 1978 and the DRCOG in 1983 and had surgical and anaesthetic training posts in various United Kingdom centres. However, in the end he settled for general practice in Tonbridge, Kent. On 7 April 1981 in St Michael's, Chester Square, London he married Anne Veronica Hickman (née Higginson), widow of Dr John Hickman, chest physician and a long-standing friend of Mark's.

Chapter 9

Honours and organizations outside the hospitals

POST-WAR HONOURS

One of the first of Ian's honorary appointments after the war was as Surgeon in Ordinary to successive Governors of Northern Ireland from 1948 to 1976. This was a new post and his war service and role in the Order of St John seem to have been the deciding factors in his appointment. His role consisted of advising the governor and his family on surgical matters and attending official functions. Ian was particularly friendly with Lord Wakehurst, who was governor from 1952 to 1964 and was Lord Prior of the Order of St John 1948–69. The actual duties of the Surgeon in Ordinary were not particularly onerous and it gave Ian great pleasure to be able to say to his assistant towards the end of an operation 'Must rush off now, John – an appointment with the Governor at 12 o'clock. Just finish the case for me.' At a reception at Hillsborough Castle in the 1980s he looked round the portraits of past Governors and, with a sweep of his hand, said 'I've taken an organ from every one of them.'

From 1956 to 1986 Ian was a Deputy Lieutenant of the City and County of Belfast. There are some 25 Deputy Lieutenants and the office involves attendance at the public functions of the city, such as Remembrance Day Ceremonies, and recommending people for honours of various kinds.

On 5 February 1963, in the middle of his year as President of the BMA, Ian was created a Knight Bachelor. The ceremony took place at Buckingham Palace and Eleanor and the children made a great family party of the occasion. Interestingly, Sir Thomas Holmes Sellors, the thoracic surgeon, was also created a Knight on the same day.

Having become a Knight of the Order of St John and now a Knight Bachelor, it seemed appropriate to Ian that he should obtain a grant of arms from the College of Heralds. His armorial bearings, granted in 1969, are as follows:

> *Arms:* Argent on a fess azure between in chief two cinque-foils gules and in base a dexter hand of the last couped at the wrist holding a strawberry plant eradicated flowered and leaved proper a sword or. *Crest:* On a wreath of the colours a stag's head cabashed proper supported on the tynes a rod of aesculapius fesswise or.
> *Motto:* Je suis prest.

There is a full list of Sir Ian Fraser's medals and academic honours in Appendix 2.

MILITARY AND POLICE BODIES

Ian was honorary consultant in surgery to the Northern Ireland Command 1948–66 and Honorary Colonel to 107 Field Ambulance (Territorial Army) 1948–67. The TA unit was based in the Victoria Barracks at that time and the post involved mainly teaching on triage, emergency care and surgery of trauma. He was also honorary colonel for ten years (1961–71) of the Number 4 (later 204) General Hospital. This was another TA unit originally based at Queen's University but which moved about 1967 to 581 Antrim Road. Here he played a similar role in training of medical officers, attending weekend and longer camps (not necessarily the whole camp) and also representing the hospital at the RAMC headquarters at Millbank. As so often, his contacts made during the war with the higher echelons of the service undoubtedly helped 204 General Hospital. Of course, his duties were not all surgical and included taking part in parades with his unit (for instance, the Queen's visit in 1950) and regular dinners, using his inimitable talents as an after-dinner speaker. Even at the age of seventy, it was not a complete retirement for he was back on many occasions until 1987 when he talked again on 'Belfast, North Africa and penicillin' (along with that other war veteran, Colonel Desmond Whyte).

The Queen's University Services Club was open to all Queen's staff, graduates and undergraduates who had served in the armed forces.

The club was formed in 1918 and from the outset always had a high proportion of medical members. There were 35 presidents in the first 50 years and 25 of them were doctors. The first two were Colonel Thomas Sinclair and Colonel Andrew Fullerton; over the years they included Dr J.S. Morrow, Sir Thomas Houston, Dr J.A. Smyth, Dr R.M. Beath, Dr Robert Marshall, Dr Ivan McCaw, Dr T.H. Crozier, Mr Ian Fraser (1954), Dr J.T. Lewis, and Mr J.R. Wheeler, all from the Royal Victoria Hospital as well as Brigadier J.A. Sinton, Major-General Brooke Purdon and Air Vice-Marshall Sir William Tyrrell. Ian was a member from his return to Belfast in 1945 and continued to be interested in it, attending the annual dinners whenever possible and proposing the health of the guests in 1978.

Yet another role taken on by Ian was as a member of the Advisory Council for the Ulster Defence Regiment. This was seen as a non-sectarian group of public-spirited men who would advise the UDR on policies, particularly on recruiting a balanced force. However, between murder and intimidation the proportion of Roman Catholics in both Council and Regiment soon declined. He was appointed in 1969 and continued to serve until he reached the age of 91 (1992).

As a result of his involvement with the UDR Advisory Council Ian was asked to be a Trustee for the UDR Benevolent Trust, which was set up in 1972. This body has inevitably had to maintain a low profile during 'the Troubles', but it exists particularly to provide help for the hundreds of disabled soldiers and their widows and children. Notoriously, the State has never treated its injured soldiers well and part-time UDR members did particularly badly. Ian was a keen and loyal Trustee in helping to raise a considerable capital fund for the UDR Trust, which had reached over £1,250,000 by the mid-1980s.

Ian's interest in these matters extended for most of his life and led him to help a much younger generation. Even as late as 1996 he was prepared to write an article for the University OTC Year Book and took the trouble to send them a photograph. This might have been considered normal and polite in his fifties, but it was truly remarkable when he had reached the age of 95.

The Northern Ireland Police Authority was formed in 1970 with Ian as its first chairman, as an attempt to represent all shades of political opinion in the policing of the province. Ian took on the task reluctantly from a feeling that he should represent balanced, non-violent opinion. He was certainly a unionist politically but did not identify with the squabbles for party advantage, unionist or nationalist, so common on such bodies. The appointment was originally for three years but Ian allowed it to be renewed, retiring from the Authority in 1976. There were many resignations and much conflict – certainly not much honour and glory to compensate for the risk. Perhaps the most worrying episode was the bombing of four homes in the Upper Malone area in 1976. The homes of Syd Scott, a property developer, Robert McCleary, auctioneer, Lady Pamela Onslow and John O'Sullivan, gynaecologist, were attacked but it was never certain whether they were specific targets or, as a headline put it, a 'Bomb Blitz on Ulster Rich'.

THE ORDER OF ST JOHN

Ian had been one of the moving spirits of the St John Ambulance Brigade and the St John Ambulance Association in the pre-war years and for his work was awarded the OBE in 1940. He was the first Commissioner of the Northern Ireland District of the Brigade 1932–9 and when he joined up his place was taken by Professor Gregg Wilson 1939–43 and then Mr W. Brennen FRCS 1943–44, followed by Dr R.W.M. Strain and Brigadier T.W. Davidson. The Ambulance Brigade in Northern Ireland was very busy during the war providing first aid training, helping to organise the Blood Transfusion Service, on duty constantly throughout the air raids of 1941 and comforting distressed relatives.

Ian, as we have seen, was admitted to the Order of St John as a Commander (Brother) in 1935 and promoted to a Knight of Grace in 1941. This is in fact the lower of the two grades of Knight within the Order, and promotion to the grade of Knight of Justice required examination of Ian's family history. He provided the necessary information and was duly re-classified as Knight of Justice in 1956, eventually being elevated to Bailiff Grand Cross in 1974. It may well be asked 'What is the Order of St John?', for to the uninitiated it would seem to be a complex body with various subsections, concerned mostly with dress and ritual and with little connection with the highly respected St John Ambulance Brigade. It traces its origin back to a hospital in Jerusalem dedicated to St John the Almoner and established even before the Crusaders entered the city in 1099. The Order was founded for the relief of suffering and when driven out of the Holy Land, transferred to Cyprus and later to Rhodes. The Order was driven out of Rhodes by the Turks in 1523 and moved to Malta, where it survived until the last Grand Master surrendered to Napoleon in 1798. The Sovereign Order later had a new beginning in Rome and survives today as a Catholic philanthropic body.

In the meantime the English branch of the Order had been suppressed by Henry VIII and was only re-founded in 1831 as a body embracing all Christian denominations. Its charitable foundations are the St John Ambulance and the Ophthalmic Hospital in Jerusalem. With this background and a long history of fighting Saracens and Turks, its appeal to both the military and the humanitarian instincts of Ian Fraser becomes clearer. Almost certainly, the other attraction of the St John Ambulance and even more of the Order of St John was the opportunity to mix with the 'great and the good'. However, rather than being too hard on this, one could argue that creating an aura of high social tone round the St John Ambulance organization brought in volunteers and generally benefited the charity in its work.

After his return from the war Ian was a founder member of the new committee of the Order for Northern Ireland in 1947. This committee, with the help of the Governor, Lord Wakehurst, who as we have seen was also Lord Prior of the Order, set about re-establishing the Commandery of the Ards, dissolved by Henry VIII in 1540. It was duly re-formed in 1952 with Lord Wakehurst as Knight Commander and Ian became a member of the chapter. Ian subsequently became Lieutenant or Deputy to the Knight Commander in 1968, serving under Lord Grey of Naunton 1970–7 and the Duke of Westminster 1977–9. He then succeeded as Knight Commander from 1979 to 1981 and, after resignation from this role, continued as a member of the Commandery Chapter, being a regular attender. Altogether it was recognized that his contribution to the development and success of St John in Northern Ireland was immense, over an unparalleled period of time from 1932 until his death. His funeral in 1999 included the considerable formalities of laying up his banner as Bailiff Grand Cross.

THE QUEEN'S UNIVERSITY OF BELFAST

Ian Fraser was elected to the Senate of Queen's in 1956 and from then on served the university in many capacities. His particular role was as non-specialist representative of the Senate on the Board of Curators from 1966 to 1988. This is a committee established by statute that advises the Senate on the appointment of professors and lecturers. These members serve for four years and it was observed that Ian, with his wide knowledge of the world and of people, could ask some very searching questions even in disciplines far removed from medicine. Finally, when he stood down from the Senate he was awarded an honorary LLD in 1992 in recognition of his services.

ROYAL BELFAST ACADEMICAL INSTITUTION ('Inst')

Ian had a long-standing affection for his old school which comes out particularly in his *Blood, Sweat and Cheers* (1989). He was elected a member of the Board of Governors as early as 1932 and after leave of absence during the war returned to the Board in 1945, resigning only in 1970. He was Visitor of the Day at the Upper School Prizegiving in 1972, giving out the prizes and making the customary speech of encouragement to the boys who didn't win a prize. In association with the prizegiving he donated an annual Ian Fraser Prize for Science. He also had a keen interest in Inst's success at rugby and took part in a curious gift/loan scheme by which the donor gave the old Instonians a cheque for (say) £50 and received in return an undated cheque from the Association for £50, which could then be dated and banked when the recipient wanted. In most instances, the cheque was never presented for payment.

THE ULSTER MEDICAL SOCIETY

Like most Ulster doctors, Ian joined the Ulster Medical Society soon after qualifying. In the 1930s he published several short papers but his main papers for the Journal came in the post-war era, including the text of his presidential address (1968). This, together with his lecture on the treasures of the Ulster Medical Society, will be discussed in the next chapter. He was elected an Honorary Fellow of the Society in 1977, 'in recognition of his outstanding professional achievements and contribution to the Society'.

THE ULSTER SURGICAL CLUB

One of Ian's major interests in the latter half of his life was the Ulster Surgical Club, of which he was president from its foundation in 1955 until his death. The club was the conception of Ronnie Loane of the South Tyrone Hospital, Dungannon, and William Hanna of the Waveney Hospital, Ballymena. They asked Ian if the thought such a club would be good for Ulster surgery and, when he was enthusiastic about it, invited him to be its first president. It was conceived on the lines of the English surgical clubs, with membership limited to about 40 (35 active members together with some retired surgeons and a small number of honorary members), entry being attained by invitees who had been duly proposed and elected. Membership was from a wide range of surgical specialities and a few others who had been invited to join.

The events usually consisted of an October meeting in Northern Ireland and a May meeting in the UK or continental Europe. Ian was always happy to ask his surgical contacts for hospitality, and the club was made welcome from Aberdeen to Athens. On every visit he was very much their leader; he always made use of career details of their hosts and always had an appropriate speech at the ready. In 1990 a new Hanna-Loane Lecture was created, to be given biennially at the home meeting. Ian was the first lecturer and spoke on Surgical Travelling Clubs, covering the subject with his usual verve and a multiplicity of slides.

THE ROYAL COLLEGE OF SURGEONS IN IRELAND

As we have seen, Ian was examiner for the RCSI before the war and was elected to its council even before his return from India, in June 1945. As a result Ian knew William Doolin, surgeon in St Vincent's Hospital, Dublin and past president of the college, sufficiently well to ask him for a reference when he applied for the Chair of Surgery in 1946. They continued to be close friends, in regular contact about college examinations, the Carmichael essay prize, etc., and William and his wife stayed with Ian and Eleanor several times in Belfast and Donegal. William Doolin was president of the college in 1952–4 and wrote to Ian early in 1952:

> The choice of Vice-President is, by tradition, in the hands of the past Presidents, on the nomination of the incoming President … You have been one of the most faithful attendants at our meetings of Council, you have never failed to bring some share of strong gaiety to our Charter Day Dinners, and you are more familiar with the Southern Schools than most of the members of Council. And, lastly, we are only too pleased to show that in our professional brotherhood we recognise no restricting boundaries! I shall be very happy to think, as time goes on, that having been instrumental in introducing you to the college via your Fellowship examination, I have had some small share in elevating you to the highest post which the College has in its gift. I am sure, too, that Eleanor will be pleased to know how much we think down here of the 'wee man' from Belfast.

In 1952 Ian was elected Vice President and in 1954 President of the Royal College of Surgeons in Ireland, and this was indeed one of the great moments of his life, following in the footsteps of his admired teacher Professor Andrew Fullerton. It was largely a period of routine in the college, the main excitement being provided by the set events, such as dinners and conferring of honorary degrees. In February 1956 Ian had the pleasure of conferring the honorary fellowship on Dr Richard Cattell, the distinguished liver surgeon from the Lahey Clinic, Boston, who had repaired Sir Anthony Eden's common bile duct, and on Sir Clement Price Thomas, of the Westminster Hospital, who had operated on King George VI.

Richard Cattell's visit to Dublin was preceded by a week in Belfast as guest of Ian and Eleanor, during which he gave the Sir Thomas and Lady Edith Dixon Lecture at the Royal Victoria Hospital on 'Advances in pancreatic surgery'. As mentioned above, one of Ian's gifts was of making friends of distinguished figures so that they could be asked to do something for the Belfast Medical School, and bringing the Director of the Lahey Clinic in Boston to lecture when he was at the height of his surgical powers is a good example. A corollary to this was that he was able to ensure an invitation for Dr and Mrs Cattell to visit Stormont as guests of the Prime Minister, Lord Brookeborough.

On a lighter note, there is an amusing exchange in 1954 between the Registrar of the College and himself: 'Do you propose to have music at the Charter Day Dinner? If so is it to be the usual Gilbert and Sullivan business? If not, what would you like?' Ian's reply is diplomatic: 'I am certainly most anxious to have music at the Charter Day Dinner, I personally enjoy greatly Gilbert and Sullivan and so, I think, will my guests from England. I do realise that the Dublin fraternity get very tired of hearing the same singers several times per week. Nigel Kinnear spoke to me about this and seemed to think that some other form of music would be preferable … I will leave it in yours and his hands, but I would like music, and it should be fairly gay.'

During the first half of the century, on average one Honorary Fellowship had been conferred every two years, but from 1950 on, certainly encouraged by Ian, there were one or two every year. These took place before the Charter Day Dinners and on other suitable occasions, and Ian's turn to deliver a citation came round fairly often. He clearly enjoyed delivering such citations, especially if he knew the surgeon in question. He always gave the impression that they were 'off the cuff' and casual, but when he said 'I do not intend to list the vast number of honorary fellowships that came his way' (Sir Harry Platt), it wasn't because he did not know of them, but because he could give a better impression of the man without them.

One of the first of Ian's citations was in 1961 for Dr Isidor Schwaner Ravdin, a surgeon from Indiana who had served in both world wars as well as being chief of surgery in Philadelphia and President of the American College of Surgeons. During the Second World War Ian had actually heard him lecture 'under the shadow of the Taj Mahal', and this must have added to his interest in the conferee.

In 1963 he delivered the citation for Professor Vasilievitch Petrovsky, director of a surgical clinic in Moscow. He certainly appealed to Ian as military surgeon, editor of a journal and internationalist, and it was not difficult for Ian to warm to his theme. In the following year it was the turn of Eric Husfeldt, described by Ian as 'the Scarlet Pimpernel of the Danish resistance movement', as well as a noted cardiac surgeon and researcher. In 1967 it was the turn of Jan Nuboer from Utrecht, Professor of

Surgery, linguist and fisherman. As Ian said diplomatically, 'We have waited 200 years to find the right man to represent Holland on our honorary roll.' Next came Professor Frank Bergan in 1968 – a Viking from the land of Thor Heyerdahl, Ibsen and Grieg. In 1969 came another Dane, Professor Orvan Swenson, a paediatric surgeon who had settled in Boston and Chicago. He was followed in 1971 by another European, Professor Philip Sandblom, a professor in paediatric cardiac surgery at Lausanne, Switzerland, who was the first surgeon in Europe to carry out the Blalock shunt.

The citation for Sir Harry Platt in 1976 gave Ian the chance to place him in the company of John Hunter and Percival Pott, who had received the fellowship 100 years earlier, and of Abraham Colles, 'the greatest of our own Irish orthopods'.

In 1977 he gave the citation for Ola Knutrud, yet another Viking who was a paediatric surgeon trained in Great Ormond Street. The fact that he was a superb skier and yachtsman and had two daughters studying in Dublin added spice to his CV. Daoud Hanania was director-general of the Royal Medical Service in Jordan, that is, the senior military surgeon of that country, and was given his honorary fellowship in 1980. Perhaps surprisingly he combined this with the speciality of cardiac surgery, having trained in St Mary's Hospital, London, the Royal College of Surgeons (of England) and Houston, Texas; Ian's citation is warm and enthusiastic.

Probably the most interesting of his assignments in delivering citations was that for the American surgeon Loyal Davis, which took place in the White House, Washington, on 14 July 1981. The occasion was unique in the history of the Irish college as the recipient was father of Nancy Reagan, wife of the President of the United States. His two medical claims to fame were as senior neurosurgeon in Chicago and long-standing editor of the journal *Surgery, Gynaecology and Obstetrics*. Ian said that Davis had been described as one of the two most eminent surgeons America had produced in the past fifty years, but the name of the other was left to the imagination.

The last citation that he delivered in Dublin was for General Doctor Isador Papo of Belgrade, Yugoslavia, in 1982. He had served with Tito's partisan forces and had practised war surgery there before training as a cardiac surgeon in Russia and the United States. As well as all this he was an incorrigible practical joker and had been created a KBE along with General Tito – truly an unusual man, and Ian had the advantage of knowing him personally.

The bicentenary of the college came in 1984 and Ian was asked to give a short address at a symposium on the occasion. He reviewed its early history, the inactivity of Trinity's medical school in the eighteenth century and the need for a new school of surgeons in Ireland. There were intermittent wars with France during the century and surgeons were needed particularly for the army, though there was little they could do with safety in civilian life. Gradually the college became one of the principal institutions of medical education in Ireland, and by the time of its bicentenary was able to make a worldwide contribution to both undergraduate and postgraduate teaching. Ian used the occasion therefore to summarize college history and to look at the problems for surgery at the present time, with the humbling reminder that 'If the surgeon today has seen further than his predecessor it is because he has been able to stand on the shoulders of the giants who preceded him.'

Ian resigned from the College Council in June 1987 and at the next meeting the president proposed that the College Medal be awarded to him in recognition of his service over 42 years.

THE BRITISH MEDICAL ASSOCIATION

Ian joined the BMA in 1928, and had his first letter published in the *British Medical Journal* in 1930. In the years that followed, before the war, he averaged one letter or paper per year in the *BMJ*, but was not otherwise involved in the BMA. After the war he was elected to the Council of the Belfast Division and became Chairman of the division in 1950. Subsequently he was elected Northern Ireland Representative to the Council of the Association, and represented the BMA on delegations to visit the Gold Coast in 1953, Canada and the USA in 1954 and Russia in 1956. The relationship culminated in his being installed as President of the BMA at the Belfast meeting in July 1962. The practice for many years has been that this nomination for office is made by the Council in London, usually choosing someone of international reputation from the city where the Annual Meeting is being held. Previous Annual Meetings had been held in Belfast in 1884, 1909 and 1937 with Professor

James Cuming as president in 1884, Professor Sir William Whitla in 1909 and Professor Robert J. Johnstone in 1937. There is no doubt that Mr Ian McClure, FRCS, gynaecologist at the Royal Victoria Hospital, was also a strong contender for election as president, but he had to be content with being local chairman.

The BMA's Annual Meeting of 1962 was certainly a highpoint in Ian's professional life and inaugurated a year of events in which he was in his element. The meeting itself lasted for eight days (19–27 July), like the pre-war meetings, and was inevitably a more expensive and opulent occasion than such meetings at the end of the century. The detailed organization fell to the general secretaries, Dr Dan Chapman and Mr Ian McClure and the Science Secretaries, Dr Gerry Nelson and Professor Richard Welbourn, and the events took place mainly at Queen's University. The first three working days consisted of the Annual Representative Meeting and were essentially medico-political. Then on Monday 23 July came the inauguration of the new president in which Sir Douglas Robb handed over the Badge of Office to Ian and Lady Robb invested Eleanor with the President's Lady's Badge. This was followed by the presidential address entitled 'Four milestones in a century'. Ian took as his milestones the social and medical changes around the four meetings of the BMA in Belfast, and on these he hung a wide-ranging survey (Chapter 10).

The four days of scientific meetings included some of the best of Belfast medicine: Professor Dick and Dr Dane on virus infections, D.A.D. Montgomery and R.B. Welbourn on the adrenal, and Louis Hurwitz on cerebrovascular insufficiency. Of the non-medical events the service in St Anne's Cathedral on Sunday 22 July was prominent, with a procession to the cathedral, lessons read by the president and the president elect and the Stanford Te Deum. The social events began with a welcome reception in the King's Hall as guests of Mr Ian McClure and the Northern Ireland Branch of the BMA, on 18 July. There were BMA dinners on 19 and 24 July as well as civic, government and university receptions. Just to prove that the whole event was not to provide mutual support for the distinguished and titled, there is an excellent photograph of Mark Fraser and friends relaxing at the civic reception. Finally there were a host of lunches and dinners for different groups, including the Order of St John and the RAMC, both dear to the new president's heart.

In 1965 one of the QA nurses from Normandy, Miss Edith Lees, who had since become matron of St Helen's Hospital, Barnsley, asked Ian to come over to present prizes to the nurses. He readily agreed to do this and gave the traditional speech in praise of nursing as a career, although it was already suffering from difficulties in recruitment. The photograph in the midst of glamorous and happy nurses indicates that he certainly enjoyed the prizegiving. His visit included staying with Dr George Neill, a friend from the Territorials, who was medical officer of health for Barnsley. As so often happens, this visit led to another, in March 1966, this time to talk to the Barnsley Division of the BMA on his trip to Russia.

In 1963 Ian published a paper in the *BMJ* on 'The discards of surgery'; he then turned his attention elsewhere for nearly 20 years until he began to publish a series of short pieces in the journal mainly under the title of Materia Non Medica. He also published his article 'Penicillin: early trials in war casualties' in the *BMJ* in 1984. This led to a letter from the editor, Dr Stephen Lock, asking Ian to take part in an ongoing series of autobiographies under the title of 'The Memoir Club'. Other people involved were such notable figures as Sir Christopher Booth (President of the Royal College of Surgeons), Professor Moran Campbell (respiratory physiologist) and Sir Douglas Black (President of the Royal College of Physicians). Ian readily agreed to the idea and in 1989 his *Blood, Sweat and Cheers* was published. It certainly fulfils the original criteria of 'something both witty and interesting'. Rather curiously, the Materia Non Medica has been used as a filler between some of the chapters, which at least means that the stories can be re-read there, for no one would ever find them in an old *BMJ*. One of Ian's last publications, like his first, was in the *BMJ* in 1992 and is an expanded account of the course he attended in Paris 65 years earlier. He has lost none of the bitter wit in his portrayal of inhumane medical practice on the continent.

BMA DELEGATIONS – GOLD COAST

In 1952 the BMA had overseas branches in most of the colonies and dominions, including ten in the various colonies of central Africa. There were about 70 BMA members in the Gold Coast and it seemed reasonable to establish a branch there. The BMA therefore invited Ian Fraser, who was at that time a member of council and had special knowledge from his stay in 1940–3, to go out on a visit to assess the practicality of forming a branch and to give some lectures there. Naturally he was pleased with the chance to revisit his wartime posting, especially as he was able to take Eleanor with him, though at his own expense.

The visit eventually took place in March 1953, by which time the BMA branch had already been formed. It turned out that there were not enough surgeons to justify specialized educational meetings, so in fact most of his meetings there were concerned with the medical administration of the colony and the decline in medical morale. By this time Nkrumah was Prime Minister and Africanization was proceeding steadily. Accra was the centre of the visit but short air trips to Kumasi and Tamale inland, and Takoradi on the coast, were included, so it was a busy fortnight. They had generous hospitality throughout, staying with Dr Eddey, the Director of Medical Services, and at Government House in Accra, as well as with various doctors in the smaller towns.

Ian wrote an account of his findings in the *BMJ* later that year. The main objective, as he saw it, was to increase the number of well-trained African doctors. This could only be done by persuading more British doctors to go out there to teach and to provide an infrastructure for the medical service, until more Africans were ready to take over. Ian was enthusiastic about the opportunities and experience available in the Gold Coast. He compared the huge surplus in trained specialists in the UK (60–70 applicants for every hospital post) with the shortage in Africa, both in hospital and in rural areas. In summary, he encouraged young men of the right type to go out, provided career opportunities in Africa were good enough to make it worth while.

The article provoked a lively correspondence in the *BMJ* including a letter from Ian's contemporary, Hugh Calwell, who had spent much of his career in Tanganyika, pointing out that a life-time career in Africa was almost impossible and the difficulties experienced in finding a post in the UK when one returned in middle life. Ian countered this by pointing out the responsibilities on both sides for making appointments of expatriates work, and came up with the further idea of short-term appointments for retired NHS consultants to help with clinical work and teaching. Many of these ideas could have worked but were blocked by hasty Africanization and the subsequent rise to power of corrupt governments in former African colonies.

NORTH AMERICA

In June 1955 the BMA helped Ian and Eleanor to make another medical tour – this time to the USA and Canada. Ian had not been in the United States previously, though he had met many American surgeons both before and during the war. They travelled in comfort by boat in those leisurely days, so effectively they had a week's cruise between Liverpool and New York before the work started. This visit was to last just over three weeks and covered the East Coast centres of Philadelphia, New York, Boston and the Mayo Clinic in Rochester before heading north to Chicago and across the frontier to Toronto and Montreal. The visit appears to have been along the usual lines, visiting operating theatres and attending 'grand rounds' and lectures in the various centres. At the Lahey Clinic, Boston he met Dr Richard Cattell, who was to be invited to the Royal College of Surgeons in Ireland in the following year. There is no record of their social activities on the tour, but with the legendary American hospitality they were certain to have been memorable.

BMA DELEGATION – USSR

One of the most interesting of Ian's foreign visits was the trip to the Soviet Union in August 1956. He went as one of seven doctors following a visit of Soviet doctors to Great Britain. The party consisted of two physicians (Sir George Pickering and Dr James Hamilton), two surgeons (Sir Geoffrey Jefferson and Ian), a radiotherapist (Dr Ralston Paterson), a general practitioner (Dr Mary Esselmont) and an interpreter (Dr Alexander Duddington). Altogether they spent three weeks in the Soviet Union, one in Moscow, one in Leningrad and Kiev, and one in Sochi. It was clearly a very intensive trip with a lot of travelling by train, visits to many different institutions and much hospitality, including a party in the

British Embassy. Hotels were good and food and drink were excessive. However, they did have time for sightseeing and were inevitably impressed by the magnificence of Leningrad.

Subsequently Ian wrote up the trip in some detail for *The Practitioner*. The article discusses medical training and general manpower distribution, surgical practice, blood transfusion and research. One of the most surprising aspects of the article, on re-reading it nearly 50 years later, is that in many respects the Soviets were doing then what we are doing now in the twenty-first century. Most notably, many of the students were married by the time they qualified, more than half were women and general practitioners generally worked in polyclinics rather than single-handed, doing little home visiting. The extent to which such changes have come to affect us in the United Kingdom is striking. However, surgery was largely carried out under local or spinal anaesthesia, even cardiac and thoracic operations, and Ian felt that this must be very unpleasant for the patient, even if it proved surgically satisfactory.

The most striking example was the total replacement of the oesophagus by a length of ileum in a boy who had developed a stricture due to swallowing caustic soda. The operation, which involved opening the abdominal cavity and tunnelling through the pleural cavity up into the neck, was carried out under local anaesthesia, and all in 90 minutes.

Blood donation was an extraordinary procedure involving two whole days off work – the first for a medical check-up, the second for the donation and recovery. Blood was taken from donors up to six times a year and donors were well paid for their contributions, as well as receiving special privileges.

The party saw the results of a variety of research projects in dogs into vascular anastomoses, major nerve repairs and, as Ian says, Pavlov's ghost could be seen everywhere. Ian wrote up the visit again later in his *Blood, Sweat and Cheers* and curiously describes another piece of research into the effects of stress on blood pressure. This was shown to them particularly for the benefit of Sir George Pickering, Regius Professor of Medicine at Oxford, who was studying hypertension. They were shown a male monkey in his cage who had been separated from his mate. She had been transferred to another cage nearby with another male monkey, leaving the first male to witness the sexual exchanges now going on. Naturally, the blood pressure of the first male rose with anger and frustration, but more interesting was the question of for how long this rise in blood pressure had to continue before it became irreversible. This research is not included in the *Practitioner* article but Ian considered it quite appropriate for the more anecdotal *Blood, Sweat and Cheers*. In general, Ian did not like experiments on animals and although he did not observe any actual cruelty (no worse than the human operations under local anaesthesia!), he makes it clear that he saw little useful outcome from the research and regarded it as unjustifiable.

He also indicates his views on research by the tale of their discussion as to whether or not the Russian women wore corsets. Mary Esselmont, pretty stout herself, was asked to carry out the necessary research by banging into as many fat Russian ladies as possible. The men felt it more appropriate that she should carry out the study. Sadly the results of the research, if ever carried out, were not written up.

It would be easy to conclude from this and other tales in Ian's memoir that the whole visit was a light-hearted jaunt, and this is true for much of Ian autobiographical writing. However, the *Practitioner* article, written shortly after the event, contains much 'meat' and serious discussion, reflecting Ian's deep interest in the training of medical students, medical practice and surgical technique.

THE ASSOCIATION OF SURGEONS

The First World War brought British surgeons together, and after the war Berkeley Moynihan was a leading spirit in forming the Association of Surgeons of Great Britain and Ireland to continue this interchange of ideas. He also appreciated that meeting French and American surgeons had been of great benefit to all during the war and, while continental travel has always been part of the experience of young doctors, international meetings would become more structured under an Association of Surgeons. Moynihan must also get the credit for promoting *The British Journal of Surgery*, first published in 1913, as the association's publication. The association very soon became a stimulus to improving the quality of training and research in the United Kingdom.

Ian had joined this august body as early as 1931, following its visit to Belfast as described above, and renewed his connections with it after the Second World War. He was elected president in 1957 in preparation for its second visit to Belfast in 1958. Many years later he was able to welcome the association again on behalf of Queen's University when it returned to Belfast in 1981. He gave an introductory talk about the university, placing it in the context of the other universities of the Kingdom, and ended in his usual witty and flamboyant manner. As well as recounting how he had joined the association by 'the tradesman's entrance' he entertained them with tales of Sir William Whitla, donor of the hall in which they were sitting. In connection with this meeting he wrote an attractive booklet entitled *The Belfast Medical School and its Surgeons*, which was circulated as a supplement to the *Ulster Medical Journal*.

THE ROYAL SOCIETY OF MEDICINE

Ian had been a Fellow of the Society and member of the surgical section for many years when he was elected to the council of the section. He was president of the section in 1962–3 and gave his presidential address on the discards of surgery (see Chapter 10).

THE SURGICAL TRAVELLERS

Ian had joined the Surgical Travellers in 1937, and we have seen that he was with them in Austria in 1938. Following the war things restarted slowly but he soon became a regular traveller, visiting Switzerland, Spain, Italy, South Africa, Yugoslavia and Greece. In his autobiography he characterizes Switzerland (admittedly in the 1950s) by a rather medieval type of mastectomy. It was in Spain that he saw a partial gastrectomy carried out under local anaesthetic on a young man, with a nun responsible for his morale, fanning him and telling him about his distinguished surgeon, Gonzales Bueno (Gonzales the Good), and the eminent visitors. When the operation was over the patient was expected to get up and walk to his bed, looking rather pale and shocked. The visit to Italy coincided with the centenary of Bassini's birth. Bassini was noted for an outmoded type of hernia repair and the occasion was used by the visitors for attributing all bad things in surgery to the various 'Bs', such as Bassini, Billroth and Battle (the incision). Unfortunately Battle's son Dickie was there and did not appreciate the joke.

There were also many visits within the UK, less exciting but perhaps more useful surgically. However, while the trips were important in broadening one's surgical knowledge, the principal value of all such gatherings is to make useful contacts, to meet the great names, and also to assess the value of their teaching and writings. In 1955 they came to Belfast, but only the menu of the dinner has survived as a record!

An example of the mixture of characters encountered in the Surgical Travellers is Fernand Orban, about whom Ian wrote on several occasions. He was born in Liège, Belgium in 1902 and became established there as a surgeon in the 1930s. In 1940 he became a member of the Anglo-Belgian Resistance and his wife Jeannot became even more involved as a link in the escape chain for Allied airmen and others. The story is so bizarre that it is best told in Ian's own words under the title 'What would Hippocrates have done?':

> One Sunday he was asked by a nice grey-haired old lady to come to her house for afternoon tea so that he could meet there a young man whom the old lady (she was the local link of the 'escape chain') would be launching on his journey down the escape route to freedom in Switzerland. One should say that each person only knew the name of the person in the next town who would supply the escapee with a safe overnight lodging.
>
> At the afternoon tea party the visitor spoke in almost impeccable English, but he did make one or two minor mistakes. One of these was when he said to the Professor, 'I will be in England in a week or two, and I could if you wish deliver a "brief" for you to a friend.' Although the professor himself spoke English with an appalling accent he had a very correct knowledge of English. The word 'brief' he knew was wrong. He realised that the man was a spy. If he was allowed to go down the escape route every person in this complicated chain would be shot or imprisoned and the whole escape line would be blown wide open. The spy must be liquidated.
>
> In his surgical team, the professor had only one assistant whom he could fully trust, and so he suggested to his registrar that he should take the visitor for a very interesting walk along a high path overlooking the Meuse and show him the sights. At one corner on this narrow track there was a sharp bend, and if the registrar could

possibly 'slip' at that point his companion could easily and 'accidentally' fall into the river. The whole affair was carried out two days later according to plan. Sadly, instead of the Meuse being in flood it was frozen over, and so, instead of being carried away, Mr X received a head injury only. He was brought into hospital and was put under the care of our own professor. After a few days it appeared he was going to make a full recovery, and so the professor suggested that a lumbar puncture might be advisable. This was done, some CSF was removed and replaced by some infected fluid. Next day the patient was considerably worse; all the team now rallied round with all the antibiotics available, but the patient finally died. It was interesting that on several occasions during this period inquiries came from the Germans regarding his progress, which proved that he was part of their team. Just before he died he admitted that he was a spy – he was in fact a citizen of a still uninvolved country.

Shortly afterwards the professor began to realise that he was now rather suspect and perhaps it might be wise if he silently slipped away. So it was soon after this that I made my first contact with him, when a foreign gentleman in a brand new RAMC uniform appeared for breakfast in the officers' mess at the Royal Herbert Hospital at Woolwich. His uniform was better than his English. From this contact a friendship of 40 years started, which ended only with his death. (Fraser 1986, 1989)

In 1945 Fernand Orban returned to Liège, where he was Professor of Surgery from 1959 to 1972. He came to Ireland frequently on fishing trips and was with the Surgical Travellers in Dublin in 1955 when he was given the Honorary Fellowship of the Royal Academy of Medicine in Ireland. He was subsequently elected an honorary FRCS and FACS as well as receiving many continental medals and honours. He died peacefully on 21 July 1981.

JAMES IV ASSOCIATION OF SURGEONS

This is a select body of senior surgeons scattered through the English-speaking world and formed to promote surgical exchange of ideas in advancing fields. Ian became a member in 1960 and over the years three Northern Ireland surgeons have held travelling fellowships – Terence Kennedy, George Johnston and Aires Barros d'Sa. The value of the fellowships resides as much in their prestige and the foreign connections they enable one to make as in their monetary value. The role of the members is therefore not only to raise funds for fellowships but also to strengthen social contacts with other members at lunches held in conjunction with the Association of Surgeons and on other occasions. Ian was later joined as a member by his colleague Ernest Morrison, and followed more recently by Colin Russell.

Chapter 10

Ian Fraser as writer and lecturer

Ian had been a prolific writer from the time when he settled into Belfast medical life. However, the pattern changed gradually, from the short case reports and reviews of the 1930s, then a natural gap in the war years and on to more didactic articles for *The Practitioner* and elsewhere in the 1950s and 1960s. From the 1950s onwards he also became more and more interested in medical history, particularly the history of surgery, of military surgery and the overlapping history of the Belfast Medical School. No fewer than 13 papers fall into this category, one of them in the *Ulster Medical Journal* running to 39 pages – possible in 1968 but certainly not to be tolerated today.

As well as the themes mentioned above, certain names keep recurring, such as Sir William MacCormac, Professor Andrew Fullerton and Robert Campbell. Most of the papers resulted from lectures to learned bodies and the interest of the organization determined the topic as, for instance, 'The heritage of the Royal Victoria Hospital' already mentioned, or the paper on John Snow to the Association of Anaesthetists, or 'The doctor's debt to the soldier' to the RAMC. He did not believe in including footnotes or even a bibliography, for the papers remained essentially as the lecture was delivered, but they all involved a considerable amount of research and it is only when they are to be used as a springboard for further research that difficulties arise. Altogether there is so much of reminiscence, research and comment in this historical group that it is well worth summarizing them.

FOUR MILESTONES IN A CENTURY (1962)

Ian took as his theme events around the three previous meetings of the BMA in Belfast (1884, 1909 and 1937) as well as current (1962) and future developments. In 1884 the medical advances were particularly significant, including Koch's identification of the tubercle bacillus (1882) and the completion of the triad that liberated surgery from its shackles: anaesthesia (1840s), antisepsis (1860s) and asepsis (1880s). The period around 1909 was one of consolidation rather than spectacular advance and Freyer reported 600 prostatectomies with only a 6 per cent mortality. The meeting was attended by four of the century's giants – Moynihan, Kocher, Osler and Almroth Wright – and the last of these declared at the meeting that 'the physician of the future will be an immunizator'. The period around 1937 was notable for the introduction of orthopaedics as a major speciality. It also saw the trial of prefrontal leucotomy – one of the many discards of surgery touched on by Ian in a whole paper in 1963.

Ian saw the era of 1962 in terms of great surgical advances that did come to stay, such as corneal grafting, middle ear surgery and full correction of congenital and acquired cardiac problems. Infectious disease had largely gone (and the horrific replacements such as AIDS and CJD had still to come). On the debit side he stresses the increase in trauma, particularly on the roads, and highlights not only the inadequate surgical resources but also our slowness in dealing with its causes. In the field of surgical provision he was indeed ahead of his time when he said that 'traumatic surgery was still to remain the Cinderella of surgery'. Of course he bemoans the decline in morals and the replacement of Royal Doulton by plastic disposables, but who can say that he was wrong? Many 'disposables' are really indestructible and pose unknown problems for the future. As always, the scientists get a dig, being described as 'untidy in dress – often neither cleanliness nor godliness obtrudes too ostentatiously'. However, all in all the address is worth re-reading for it does identify much of the best and worst of medicine, and the problems have not gone away.

THE DISCARDS OF SURGERY (1963)

This was a subject that had fascinated Ian for many years – operations that were highly popular or could be described as fashionable for a few years and were then abandoned. He was certainly tormenting librarians in Britain and the USA a year before his talk was to be given, and returned to the theme in his autobiography (1989). He chose the subject for his presidential address to the Surgical Section of the Royal Society of Medicine and it was published in the *BMJ* in 1963. His theme is that what makes surgery interesting is the possibility that one can go wrong – make the wrong diagnosis, perform the wrong operation – or, more optimistically, try out a better operation or new instrument. In the case of instruments, many were invented for particular situations e.g. the Reverdin needle used by the French because they wore stiff rubber gloves when operating. Complicated and varied retractors were necessary in the absence of surgical assistants or relaxation of the abdominal muscles by the anaesthetist. The tongue forceps, which gripped the tongue by crushing it, were discarded when airway management by the anaesthetist improved.

Pre-operative procedures had become simpler since the introduction of antibiotics. Skin preparation and shaving was less drastic. Dental treatment was no longer regarded as an essential preliminary. Early ambulation and early return to oral fluids had certainly become quite acceptable by the 1960s.

Some operations had disappeared because they were no longer necessary, such as the surgery of tuberculosis, which happily had been overcome by the 1960s. The surgery of osteomyelitis had been superseded by antibiotics, and that of renal failure by renal dialysis. Symphthectomies for hypertension and for peripheral vascular disease, and also prefrontal leucotomy, had disappeared with the advent of specific drugs. Other procedures such as the '-pexies' went because they were never necessary in the first place, such as nephropexy and caecopexy.

When Ian talks of 'discarded attitudes' he is probably being optimistic – as a president has to be. There is still acrimony and jealousy between colleagues in hospital, and there are still surgeons who exaggerate the success of their surgery and turn a blind eye to their failures. With his instinctive dislike of animal experimentation, Ian is at pains to point out how misleading it can be, as seen in O'Shaunessy's cardio-omentopexy, which did marvels for the cardiac vascularity of fit greyhounds but nothing for the fibro-fatty heart of the patient with myocardial ischaemia. We are probably not going to repeat the same mistakes as our forefathers but the paper is a reminder that evaluation of surgical procedures cannot be foolproof and that current operations will in many cases be replaced by new ones or obviated by new drugs.

THE DOWNE HOSPITAL BICENTENARY (1967)

Ian had a strong affection for the Downe Hospital ever since he did a locum there in the 1920s to allow Dr J.C. ('Jack') Robb to get married. Even with the advent of the Health Service the hospital did not change very much, with its resident surgeon in charge of everything, helped by the occasional visiting physician, gynaecologist and anaesthetist, much of the work still being done by house surgeons of several years' standing and all the staff with an abiding loyalty to the institution. In addition, Ian had known Dr Robb's successor, Mr J.S. ('Johnny') Boyd, for many years and felt that he followed in 'Jack' Robb's footsteps as a surgeon with a truly wide range of skills, if necessary acting as physician or obstetrician.

Ian was therefore very pleased when asked to take part in the bicentenary celebrations of the Hospital in 1967, by delivering a historical lecture that was a broad picture of medicine over the two centuries, particularly the decline of infectious diseases, development of effective drugs and the facilitation of safe surgery by anaesthesia, antisepsis and asepsis. It was the first of his historical lectures/papers after his retirement and, while he continued with private practice, he naturally had much more time for reading and research. Specifically of Downpatrick interest there were many pioneers and characters. Dr John Maconchy, the resident surgeon, was the first surgeon in Ireland to report the use of Lister's method of antisepsis, in 1868. He had sent his assistant, Dr Edwin Nelson, to see Lister working in Glasgow and had been practising the technique in Downpatrick for nine months.

Dr Joseph Nelson, Edwin's brother, earned his fame outside Downpatrick but both were sons of the non-subscribing Presbyterian minister, the Rev. Samuel Craig Nelson, a member of the extensive Nielson family. In the 1860s, in the middle of his medical course at Queen's, Joseph went off to join Giuseppe Garibaldi's 'red shirts' in Genoa. He campaigned with the famous Regimento Inglese through Sicily and Italy and took part in the battle of Volturno, receiving the sword of honour and medals commemorating the campaign.

The third personality described in the lecture was another hospital surgeon, Dr Thomas Tate, who ruled at Downpatrick from 1892 to 1926. Ian describes two of Dr Tate's cases in which he made the diagnosis against opposition from outside specialists and proved himself right by surgery on the spot. The first was a Colonel Edward Sanderson MP who took ill with a chest problem and fever, in the Slieve Donard Hotel. Dr Tate diagnosed an empyema (pus round the lung), proved it with a small needle and finally put in a large drain to remove 1–2 pints of pus. The other involved Stephen Perceval Maxwell, who developed sudden abdominal pain at the age of 58. Surgeon Tate came up with the totally obscure diagnosis of a hernia of the small intestine through the foramen of Winslow and demonstrated the truth of his diagnosis to a sceptical Professor Sinclair. The anaesthetic was given by Dr Charles Dickson, who vouched for the details to Ian, and the case was written up in the *BMJ* in 1909 by Professor Sinclair, giving full credit for the diagnosis to Surgeon Tate.

Ian's relationship with 'Johnny' Boyd was long and he felt that it would be interesting to arrange a small exhibition to show 200 years of surgery at the Downe. The first problem was to collect material for the exhibition; this was done by the two of them setting off to London and visiting the various medical museums. Thanks to the strength of Ian's personality and contacts they were able to borrow the necessary items with a minimum of fuss.

The trip was completely successful but when they were in BMA House Ian recalled a curious incident later described by John Boyd in a note to the *BMJ* (1995):

As we passed through a small courtyard he talked for a short time about a very ordinary looking fish pond which contained some ordinary looking fish. Eventually he spotted something which he had obviously been looking for – a collection of small ordinary looking trees. From amongst this collection he selected one mundane looking specimen. 'That,' said Sir Ian, 'is a very interesting and unique tree.' I could not see anything distinctive or interesting about the tree and I said so. However I excused my ignorance by declaring that I was no horticultural expert. In his own inimitable way Sir Ian stroked the foliage with such care and reverence that I almost felt obliged to genuflect on the spot. He continued, 'During my term as president I was one morning alone in my office when a knock came to the door. On my invitation two bronzed young men entered. They then proceeded to inform me that they had been sent by the citizens of the island of Kos. The visitors went on to explain that the people of Kos (birthplace of Hippocrates) would deem it a great honour if their two ambassadors were permitted to plant a tree in the grounds of the relatively new BMA establishment. Sir Ian naturally thought that the idea was an excellent one and immediately set about arranging a planting ceremony. On an agreed time and date the two men arrived accompanied by a man with a spade and a photographer.

Sir Ian then appeared with a party of top BMA officials, all dressed in morning suits and bowler hats. As the small tree was lowered ceremoniously into a prepared hole the BMA deputation doffed their bowlers to the accompaniment of clicking cameras. Then with that whimsical Fraserian smile Sir Ian continued, 'We are not sure where those gentlemen came from, but we are now sure that they did not come from Kos, and we strongly suspect that there are now, somewhere in the world, a few doctors who as medical students fooled their superiors. They got away with a set of valuable and embarrassing photographs while we are left with that very ordinary tree which was probably stolen from a public park.'

JOHN SNOW AND HIS SURGICAL FRIENDS (1967)

The lecture was given as the John Snow Lecture when the Association of Anaesthetists visited Belfast in 1967. Ian compared John Hunter, in particular, with Snow but also ranged over Joseph Lister, Sir William Fergusson, Sir James Young Simpson and many others. Of course he exhibited his prejudices in favour of old-fashioned simple medicine. It would astonish anaesthetists now to hear Ian praising them for using methods of monitoring such as the hand on the pulse and the stethoscope, while avoiding the ECG.

Ian made extensive use of John Snow's diaries, covering some 4,285 cases, anaesthetized with chloroform without a death. Clearly the case books are at least as interesting to the surgeon as to the anaesthetist, and should be better known to the social historian. The paper is full of admiration for Snow, for his energy in innovation as well as the routine and for his success in working with all the surgeons of London in this ten-year period. Sadly, Ian wondered whether we have lost the great surgical 'characters' of Snow's day and, if so, was it because anaesthetists had made surgery too easy. With hindsight we can be sure that neither of these suggestions was true.

FATHER AND SON – A TALE OF TWO CITIES (1968)

Several papers cover Ian's surgical predecessors in Belfast from different points of view, as has been mentioned in Chapters 2 and 3. The most valuable of these historical studies is that of Sir William MacCormac, Ian's presidential address to the Ulster Medical Society in 1967. The interest of the paper is also in its account of Sir William's father, Professor Henry MacCormac, and the contrast Ian draws between the physician and the surgeon – the one of Belfast and the other mainly of London, both on the staff of the Belfast General Hospital and each very successful in his sphere. Ian's papers rarely contain detailed references to their sources, but certainly the value of this study was in its access to the family papers, diaries and letters.

Henry MacCormac (1800–71) was born in County Armagh, graduated MD at Edinburgh and then spent a year travelling in West Africa. What was of special interest to Ian was that he visited the Gold Coast, and indeed wrote about it many years later. Two of Henry's brothers settled in West Africa and a niece married an African called Easmon, starting a small dynasty of doctors in the area, one of whom became the Chief Medical Officer in Ghana. Henry later travelled to Canada and the USA before marrying and settling down as Professor of Medicine at the Belfast 'Inst' Medical School. He held the chair from 1837 to 1849 but was not appointed professor in the new medical school of Queen's College. In spite of this and his eccentricity, he contributed greatly to the care of the sick in the Belfast General Hospital, the asylum and in private practice.

Henry's son William MacCormac (1836–1901) was much closer to Ian's ideal. After qualifying at the Queen's University in Ireland in 1857 he was appointed visiting surgeon to the General Hospital in 1864. He then eloped with and married Katherina, daughter of John Charters, a rich linen merchant and subsequently a benefactor of the General Hospital. Instead of settling down at this stage he decided to go off to care for the wounded in the Franco-Prussian War in 1870. The experience he obtained after the battle of Sedan, with its 12,000 casualties, obviously struck a chord with Ian's experience at Bayeux, though under much less satisfactory conditions.

Subsequently William MacCormac decided to move to London, where he was able to get on to the staff of St Thomas's Hospital. He later threw himself into the Turko-Serbian war and the Boer War and did much to raise the standard of military surgery and care of the wounded. William was clearly a very successful surgeon and on the basis of the diaries he comes across as flamboyant rather than eccentric, and prosperous without being greedy. In 1896 he was elected President of the Royal College of Surgeons, and having already been given a knighthood, in 1897 he was made a baronet and in 1900 he received the KCVO and the KCB. His greatest professional success was as an ambassador for British surgery but for all this success, his private affection for his wife, 'dear Kate', and his many dogs brings him very close to us. Throughout the long paper we can see why Ian had a special admiration for Sir William and in the end appears closer to him than to his teacher, Andrew Fullerton.

Ian returned to this topic in his Thomas Vicary Lecture, given at the Royal College of Surgeons of England in 1982.

MEDICAL ADVANCES SINCE THE TIME OF BISHOP JEREMY TAYLOR (1970)

This is perhaps the broadest of Ian's sweeps into medical history, in which he addresses an audience of clergy on developments over three centuries. Jeremy Taylor was Bishop of Dromore in the period after the restoration of Charles II in 1660, and is noted for his purging the

Church of all elements of presbyterianism that had crept in during the Commonwealth period. He died of 'fever' at his home in Lisburn in 1667, presumably typhoid or typhus fever, both of which were regularly fatal. His wife and five of their children had already died of tuberculosis or smallpox. He was also affected by the deaths of a mother and child in the household where he was sheltering during the Commonwealth, and under the influence of these disasters he wrote his most celebrated work, *Holy Dying*. This experience of deaths in past centuries from infection and childbirth forms the theme of Ian's talk.

Ian makes the point that the striking advances over the centuries have been in the overcoming of these causes of death and the improvement of our understanding of cause and effect so that we no longer blame witches for disease or attempt to cure it by bleeding the patient to death. These were not the only hazards to the sick in the eighteenth century, for the hospitals were a breeding ground for infection, nurses were dirty and drunken, patients slept many in a bed and alcohol was given freely to anyone over eight years of age. Advances often came about as the result of chance or what we like to call serendipity, notably in the American Indians' discovery of the benefits of quinine and Fleming's observations of the penicillin fungus. Once again Ian highlights the three 'A's of surgery – anaesthesia in the 1840s, antisepsis in the 1860s and asepsis in the 1880s – and points out, as we shall see below, that wars were a potent stimulus to advances in surgery and nursing. Reading the typescript, for the lecture was never printed, one can see why Ian was so successful as a teacher of students, doctors and the wider public.

THE DOCTOR'S DEBT TO THE SOLDIER (1971)

The next historical lecture, given three years later, has similar resonances to the one dealing with Sir William MacCormac, as it concerns a surgeon who made his name at least partly in the wars and was also on the staff of St Thomas's Hospital. Ian had met Philip Mitchener initially with the Surgical Travellers and during the Second World War in England and North Africa, appreciating his Rabelaisian humour as much as his contributions to surgery in a famous textbook. However, Mitchener's life, with its exciting and generously given service in Serbia, was only the starting point for a picture of how surgical advances had derived from military conflict.

The Crimean war saw the introduction of ether anaesthesia by both British and French armies, in spite of the statement by Dr John Hall that ' the knife is a powerful stimulant and it is much better to hear a man howl lustily than to see him sink silently into his grave'. Plaster-of-Paris also came into widespread use, particularly by the Russian surgeon Pirogoff. Thirdly, of course, Florence Nightingale gave nursing a new status and shamed the government into doing something for the care of the wounded.

The Franco-Prussian war strictly did not involve Britain, but some 62 British surgeons and 18 nurses travelled to give their services to the forerunner of the Red Cross Society. One of these was the young William MacCormac of Belfast; his commanding officer was the American gynaecologist Marion Sims. As Ian says to his military audience, 'It must be a relief for a gynaecologist to get a chance to do a bit of honest surgery'. MacCormac took over command when Sims returned home and the war, along with contacts with the well-organized Prussian army, eventually helped to bring about the establishment of the RAMC.

Medical services in the army were therefore much better by the time the South African war broke out in 1899. Nevertheless, when MacCormac again went out to the front he reported on the lack of forward casualty clearing units, disastrous when road transport was almost impossible. The main lessons learned here were on sanitation and hygiene generally, but the greatest outcome was the introduction of inoculation against typhoid fever by Almroth Wright, though it was put into operation fully only in 1914.

The First World War also saw the introduction, belatedly, of the Thomas splint, invented as far back as 1878 but not really used for more than 30 years. Unfortunately blood transfusion, although the various blood groups had been identified from the beginning of the century, had not yet become practical and really had to await the Second World War. In the interval the value of plasma was learned in the Spanish Civil War. Tetanus toxoid also came in with this war. The other medical benefits of the two world wars have been described above, but all contribute to a fascinating paper, of which these points are only the highlights.

THE CAMPBELL HERITAGE LIVES ON (1973)

Ian had long admired Robert Campbell as one of the pioneers of paediatric surgery in the Belfast Hospital for Sick Children. He was appointed assistant surgeon there in 1897 and died in 1920 at the early age of 57. Ian could never have known him, although, as we have seen, he was a close friend of Ian's father and sufficient folklore about him had survived to make him a worthy hero to emulate. Robert Campbell was a progressive surgeon in all fields and introduced to Belfast the use of rubber gloves for operating, but his special contribution was operating to repair inguinal hernias in infancy rather than at the age of 6–10 years. This avoided the use of a dirty truss throughout childhood and removed the worry of strangulation. Campbell's paper of 1907 described 1,500 cases with only one death, and that was due to delayed chloroform poisoning.

Campbell did a prodigious amount of work both in the daytime and on emergencies, but his other original contribution was to pioneer operations on outpatients. Of course Ian touches on his regular themes – the lack of payment for the attending staff, the poverty of the whole hospital and the follies of Surgeon Kirk!

THE TREASURES OF THE ULSTER MEDICAL SOCIETY (1978)

This is the title of a talk Ian gave to the society in 1978 but never published. He made an attempt to get it into the *Ulster Medical Journal* in 1985 but it was clearly too long and the editor (David Hadden) felt that much was irrelevant or was taken from previous publications in the journal, particularly Bill Strain's paper of 1967. However, the subject made an excellent talk and the typescript is still 'a good read'. Ian describes the origins of the society from the union in 1862 of the Belfast Medical Society (founded in 1806) and the Belfast Clinical and Pathological Society (founded in 1853). He goes on to outline the role of Sir William Whitla in presenting it with a home – the Whitla Medical Institute, sadly to be sold to Inst for demolition.

Probably the most interesting parts of the lecture are the biographies of the personalities commemorated by the society. First there was Sir William Whitla, known of course to Ian as one of his teachers, and we have here the personal anecdotes rather than the dry bones – the question of how he made his money, his views on the design of the Royal Victoria Hospital, his interest in the Book of Daniel, and his lonely old age. Sir William's bust is one of the treasures of the society, and some years later Professor W.W.D. Thomson presented a portrait of Sir William painted posthumously by Frank McKelvey (photographic copy in the Royal Victoria Hospital).

In 1904, on the occasion of the presentation of the bust of Sir William Whitla, it was commented that Edward Jenner had probably done more for the health of mankind than any other known person. This stimulated Sir Otto Jaffé (Lord Mayor) to offer to present a portrait of Jenner. Ian was a great admirer of Jenner, and in the lecture gives quite a lot of space to him and his career.

Another of the great historical characters commemorated, and this time a genuine Ulsterman, was Sir Hans Sloane. Professor Thomson thought the society should remember him, and decided to have a copy of Stephen Slaughter's portrait made for the society. Ian outlines his career from his birth in Killyleagh to medical success and wealth in London – wealth that enabled him to build up a very broad collection which eventually became the basis of the British Museum.

A major and distinctive gift to the society from Sir William Whitla was the window in the Institute commemorating Dr William Smyth of Burtonport, who died of typhus caught while tending the sick on the island of Arranmore. The Ulster Medical Society also has a portrait of Professor Alexander Gordon presented by his daughter, although Ian makes it clear that he thinks that Whitla overrated Gordon's skills.

Sir Robert Johnstone is commemorated by a fine portrait by Frank McKelvey He was one of Ian's teachers as Professor of Gynaecology, and became President of the Ulster Medical Society (1922–3), President of the BMA (1937–8) and MP for Queen's University (1921–1938). He seems to have been good at everything he touched, but perhaps one warms particularly to his talent for writing humorous poetry on medical subjects.

Finally, among the portraits, is Joseph Nelson, son of a Presbyterian minister in Downpatrick, soldier with Garibaldi's Red

Shirts, doctor to a tea plantation in India and Belfast's first eye specialist. The talk was made particularly interesting (but less publishable) by a considerable sketch of the life of Garibaldi. Strictly, he had nothing to do with the Ulster Medical Society, but one can see how he appealed to the poor and the young, not only of Italy but in England. In Ireland, however, this was counterbalanced by his fight against the papal armies, and there were placards in Hydepark reading 'No Garibaldi – Pope for Ever'. There are other portraits and many photographs of early presidents of the Society, but Ian wisely confined himself to the most colourful group.

DISEASE IS GOOD FOR YOU (1978)

This is a long lecture which was rewritten for the *Ulster Medical Journal* in 1978. The perverse title of course highlights the concept that certain people's genius has flourished under the influence of certain diseases. The particular diseases that he highlights, tuberculosis and syphilis, have virtually died out but there is sufficient documentation to support his general thesis. He makes it clear that all disease is not good, for example Neville Chamberlain's colostomy, or Anthony Eden's cholangitis, and certainly disease really only benefits those who work creatively, as distinct from the politician, the business tycoon or the university professor. (There are a few swipes at the professor with the slide rule, clearly referring to Graham Bull, and at Professor William Whitla, who claimed to be able to hear a heart murmur four beds away.)

He quotes extensively from writers such as Professor George Pickering, W.R. Bett and Dr Rentchnick of Geneva, who tried to prove that nearly any condition, ranging from hypertension to illegitimacy, could be associated with great achievements. In fact, these studies merely prove that disease and loss of a parent are very common and that there is no single thread in the observations. Even the often suggested relationship between syphilis (particularly GPI) and creative originality is probably invalidated by the great number of examples and their diversity.

The study does however give Ian an opportunity to recount many GPI stories. There was a farmer in County Londonderry who had picked up the spirochaete while he was a student in Edinburgh:

He was happily married, and on the day before I saw him he told his wife that he was going to the local fair to buy some 20–30 cattle. Some hours later she was somewhat disturbed when she saw some 300 head of cattle being driven into the yard, and when he returned in the evening he told her that this was just the beginning and he hoped to have 2,000 or 3,000 more tomorrow. The onset of his grandiose delusions had been very rapid – he was in a Belfast nursing home next day, and in Purdysburn Hospital a few days later.

Altogether the paper shows that even outside Ian's home ground of surgery he could give a broadly entertaining and irreverent view of the human condition.

THE TRAINING OF A SURGEON (1979)

This was the David Torrens lecture given at the New University of Ulster, in Ballymoney, to commemorate one of the distinguished medical graduates from the area. David Torrens had been born in Moneydig in 1897, had graduated at Trinity College Dublin, and had eventually become professor of physiology and dean of the medical school there. He was known as a humble and generous man, fond of simple pleasures like walking in the mountains and skilled in practical activities such as watch repairing and making gadgets. Since this was the first lecture in his memory, Ian paid a special tribute to him but then moved on to his own theme, which naturally included much reflection on his own training. On the debit side there was the concentrated attachment to one surgical teacher, the very low pay, and the certainty of bias in the appointment system. On the credit side there was the huge amount of experience one attained, though this was largely unsupervised and limited by the working range of one's chief.

The advent of the Health Service in 1948 brought many benefits; for training it meant the possibility of surgical rotation without close dependence on a single teacher for one's skills. It also gave the trainee a chance to visit the USA or the Third World for a year, almost unheard of in the 1920s and 1930s. It introduced the possibility of research into the training period, though it pushed there some unwilling or unsuitable young men, with the threat of 'publish or perish'. This gave Ian a chance also to comment on the professor who was expected to be a brilliant surgeon and researcher and teacher, as well as an opportunity to attack the excessive amount of animal experimentation going on.

It must be said that in many ways Ian did not see the true situation when he compared the unsupervised toil of the trainee or assistant surgeon before the National Health Service with the skilled team afterwards. It was really only the increasing specialization and fear of litigation in the 1980s that made available skilled surgeons to help their juniors for emergency work.

In his wide-ranging assessment of the state of training and the profession generally, he talks about the growing expansion of anaesthesia, moving towards its own Royal College, which he does not support (and many anaesthetists did not agree with either). He talks about the shape of the training pyramid and welcomes the fact that it is no longer necessary for so many trainees to emigrate. Postgraduate examinations have probably remained much the same over the years but the pass rate has improved with better teaching. Higher professional training has been introduced to the benefit of everyone, and junior doctors' pay has been greatly improved. All in all, Ian can view the training situation positively, though he admits that vigilance is necessary to avoid repeating the mistakes of yesterday.

THE BAD OLD DAYS – OR WERE THEY? (1983)

This was the Presidential Address to the Medico-Legal Society and it was never published – presumably because Ian felt that it contained nothing really new. However, it takes the unusual line for a man in his eighties that however bad the Health Service and our state of health appear today, things were far worse when he was a student. It is a point of view as refreshing in the twenty-first century as in the 1980s.

He compares both doctors' pay and hospital funding before 1948, and shows how poor and uncertain they were. He describes the vagaries of the appointments system and the nepotism in medical appointments to the Royal Victoria Hospital (another reason for not publishing the address!). Most forcibly of all, he details the medical advances over the past 60 years – the cures for pernicious anaemia, diabetes and tuberculosis, and the widespread applications and benefits of penicillin and DDT. Of course he talks of the high cost of coronary artery surgery and renal transplants, but defies anyone to say that we were better off without them.

The increasing specialization in medicine has always been ridiculed, and Ian recounts how a general surgeon returned to Belfast after a period of training in London. While there he had also learned a new and clever technique for removal of the tonsils. One of the ENT surgeons resented this and asked the chairman of the medical staff to intervene and stop this unfair encroachment on his territory. The chairman of staff was a gynaecologist, and replied 'You know that there are five orifices in the human body at the disposal of the marauding surgeon. The ENT surgeons have commandeered three of these, leaving one for the general surgeon and one for the gynaecologist. I do not intend to interfere if the general surgeon makes an occasional sally into your department.'

Of course, Ian realizes that many so-called advances in medicine and surgery have eventually been consigned to the dustbin – but this has always been so, and is part of the cost of medical progress. With equal justice, he points out that some of the modern panic over AIDS is engendered by the media, disregarding the much more widespread killers such as the motor car and lung cancer.

Finally, Ian quotes the remark of a Boston surgeon that 'of all the modern advances 50 per cent will be discarded in ten years from now, but the tragedy today is that we do not know which half to discard'.

Chapter 11

Growing old

As people grow older, most begin to fear the thought of severe physical or mental disability that will cloud their last years and gradually take away all the pleasure of living. Ian was fortunate in that such problems did not affect him until the last months of his long life. He enjoyed surgery and, after he retired from hospital work, continued operating well into his seventies. Perhaps even more, he enjoyed meeting people, and for this reason he kept up a private consulting practice into his nineties. After the family moved to 19 Upper Malone Road in 1951 Ian had rooms at 35 Wellington Park and there he saw his private patients right through until about 1985. There also was based his long-term secretary, Joan Sayers, who not only sorted out his appointments but typed his letters and many historical papers. Even when he gave up 35 Wellington Park he continued to see patients.

Throughout his retirement Ian kept up contact with the Royal Victoria Hospital and Royal College of Surgeons, with an active medical input at least into his seventies. Involvement with these as well as the university and all the bodies discussed earlier gradually declined or became social rather than active committee work. However, when he went to events he did not sit in a corner waiting to be noticed. At the Royal Victoria Hospital dinners he always made a short and witty speech about the loving cup and the ideas and practices of Surgeon Kirk. In Dublin, when attending an official function in the college, he appeared with past president's badge and all his military medals, saying to a colleague from the North, 'I don't know whether it's appropriate to wear these medals here – but I'm wearing them anyway.' Needless to say, it was perfectly acceptable in the college and he was always welcome, with or without medals.

It would be wrong to think of Ian as involved only in medical work. He remained fond of golf throughout middle life and took a keen interest in the garden of 19 Upper Malone Road. However, it must be said that his gardening was not exactly 'hands on'. Rather it consisted of looking at the plants and making suggestions to Eleanor and the gardener.

As the years went on Ian kept reasonably active by walking with Rory (the griffon terrier seen in Carol Graham's 1994 portrait). This would be either round the block, which kept him in touch with the neighbours, or in Dixon Park, when Joan Sayers was available to give him a lift there. Ian stopped driving in his mid-nineties and Joan Sayers took on the role of chauffeur for his many daytime activities as his need for secretarial help diminished. In the evenings Paul and Valerie Osterberg and John and Iris Weaver were staunch friends for both the medical and the purely social functions.

Indoors, when he was not writing he was involved in collecting. A stamp collection gathered during his active life was eventually sold. The bleeding bowls were given away at his 80th birthday celebrations, but antiques generally he always collected and he was devoted to the *Antiques Roadshow* on television. The collections included coins, furniture, paperweights and Irish silver, and they survived to be passed on to his children.

More social activities always dominated Ian's interest, ranging from going to the theatre, opera (especially Gilbert and Sullivan) and ballet, to entertaining and being entertained to dinner. Eleanor was never quite as sociable as Ian, but with plenty of domestic help she was an excellent hostess for their many parties at home and beyond. She was much happier in the company of their close friends, playing bridge with the Osterbergs and others, or just chatting.

Once the children went away to school in England, home was inevitably quieter, but Una Davidson remained and there were always plans for entertaining and for the children's holidays. Family holidays were in Donegal when they were small but later spread out to Majorca, Guernsey and France, with the Surgical Travellers providing more sophisticated trips abroad for Ian and Eleanor. Both Mary Alice and Mark settled down and married in England but it was easy for Ian and Eleanor to get over to see them, and once the grandchildren arrived both were enthusiastic in their attentions.

Foreign holidays continued in the 1980s, either staying in a villa in the south of France with Mark, Veronica and family or taking a comfortable cruise liner.

However, this calm pattern of life had to be interrupted by some ill health, and angina became more limiting. Ian consulted Drs John Weaver and Jennifer Adgey and it was decided in 1988 that he needed a coronary artery bypass. This was carried out in the Royal Victoria Hospital by Mr Hugh O'Kane with Dr Morrell Lyons as anaesthetist. Inevitably it caused considerable excitement in the cardiac unit, as no one expected Ian to be an easy patient. In the event he took the whole thing in his stride, was charming to everyone and was out of hospital within ten days.

Eleanor was equally fortunate in her eighties, though poor eyesight did restrict her domestic activities a little. Her one brush with the surgeons was following an accident in the concourse of Heathrow when she was knocked down and fractured her femur. Ian did his best to manage the situation in military fashion, though poor Eleanor suffered quite a lot on the plane back to Aldergrove. The last straw was when an ambulance strike left her with only the family car for transport, but thanks to Paul Osterberg the fracture was pinned and she was soon back on her feet.

Eleanor died on 30 October 1992 a few hours after a severe stroke, and it must be said that it was a merciful way to go. Ian was still active but was never a very domesticated man and certainly was glad to have one good meal a day cooked for him by Una Davidson or some alternative help. He continued to attend social and medical dinners with all his old friends and continued to have holidays with Mary Alice and Mark anywhere from Paris to Rathmullan. Then in 1998 it became evident that he was failing. More help was needed in the house, and on 11 May 1999 he died at home at the age of 98.

Eleanor and Ian were buried in the little graveyard at Drumbeg beside the old parish church, in the same grave as their baby son who had died in 1938. They have the striking and appropriate epitaph:

> From quiet homes and first beginning
> Out to the undiscovered ends
> There's nothing worth the wear of winning
> But laughter and the love of friends.

Ian was commemorated by a memorial service in Fisherwick Presbyterian Church, the church packed with many of his former friends, colleagues, nurses and those he had taught. A masterly tribute was delivered by Sir Peter Froggatt, which was later published in the *Ulster Medical Journal*. In it he quotes Ian's own statement from his autobiography: 'I have had one of the happiest lives that any man could wish for'.

This is certainly believable, for he seems to have been successful in every facet of his life. He was happily married and lived to see his children successful and also happily married. His career in hospital, in the army and in the broadest administrative field was brilliant. Finally, he will be remembered as one of the most charismatic teachers of the Belfast Medical School.

Appendix 1

Published writings of Sir Ian Fraser

Fraser, I. 'Prolapse of the rectum in children' [letter]. *British Medical Journal*, 1930; 1: 104–7.

'A rare neck cyst.' *British Journal of Surgery*, 1930; 18: 338–9.

'Purpura simulating the acute abdomen.' *Lancet*, 1930; 2: 525.

'Foreign body in the vagina' [letter]. *British Medical Journal*, 1930; 2: 308.

'Rupture of the spleen.' *Clinical Journal*, 1930; 59: 439–41.

'Cancer of the mouth.' *British Dental Journal*, 1930; 51: 1270–81.

'The cotton-wool sandwich.' *The Medical Press*, 1930; 158: 435–6.

'Septicaemia from minor wounds' [letter]. *British Medical Journal*, 1931; 1: 242.

'A very large bursa' [letter]. *Lancet*, 1932; 1: 290–1.

'Diverticulitis of the colon.' *Ulster Medical Journal*, 1932; 1: 99–104.

'Ectopic kidney' [letter]. *British Medical Journal*, 1932; 1: 128.

'Thyroid extract and pulmonary embolus' [letter]. *British Medical Journal*, 1932; 1: 659.

'The treatment and prognosis of acute osteomyelitis.' *Ulster Medical Journal*, 1933; 2: 303–7.

'An unsuspected foreign body in the hand.' *Lancet*, 1933; 2: 921.

'Diverticula of the small intestine' [letter]. *Lancet*, 1933; 2: 1291.

'The diverticula of the jejuno-ileum.' *British Journal of Surgery*, 1933; 21: 183–211.

'Towels for prostatectomy' [letter]. *British Medical Journal*, 1933; 1: 277.

'Acute appendicitis, some mistaken diagnoses.' *British Medical Journal*, 1933; 1: 310–1.

'Diagnosis of acute appendicitis' [letter]. *British Medical Journal*, 1933; 1: 540.

'Fragilitas ossium tarda.' *British Journal of Surgery*, 1934; 22: 231–40.

'The treatment of varicose veins.' *Ulster Medical Journal*, 1935; 4: 105–12.

'The injection treatment of varicose veins.' *Clinical Journal*, 1936; August.

'Note on Steinach II operation for the enlarged prostate.' *Ulster Medical Journal*, 1937; 6: 56–9.

'The International Society of Surgery.' *Ulster Medical Journal*, 1939; 8: 46–7.

'Foreign bodies.' *British Medical Journal*, 1939; 1: 967–71.

'Sarcoma of the prostate in children.' *Irish Journal of Medical Science*, 1939: 330–3.

'Recurrent intussusception in a young child.' *Lancet*, 1939; 1: 874–5.

'Avulsion of stomach from duodenum.' *Journal of the Royal Army Medical Corps*, 1940: 383–6.

'Precocious puberty in a boy of one year.' *British Journal of Surgeons*, 1940; 27: 521–6.

'Forward surgery.' *Ulster Medical Journal*, 1944; 13: 150–5.

'Penicillin.' *Irish Medical Directory and Hospital Year Book*, 1946: 37–44. Dublin.

'The treatment of haemorrhoids.' *The Practitioner*, 1952; 169: 499–504.

'The heritage of the Royal Victoria Hospital.' *Ulster Medical Journal*, 1952; 21: 114–29.

'Shortage of medical officers in the Gold Coast.' *British Medical Journal*, 1953; 2: 987–8.

[Paper on genito-urinary emergencies.] *Journal of the Irish Medical Association*, 1954; 35: 236–40.

'Medical needs in the Gold Coast' [letter]. *British Medical Journal*, 1954; 1: 214.

'Tumours of the small intestine' [abstract]. *British Medical Journal*, 1955; 2: 51.

'Argentaffinoma (Carcinoid tumour) with cyanosis.' *Lancet*, 1955; 2: 174–5.

Fraser, I. and McCredie, J.A. 'The decrease in surgical paediatric death rate.' *British Medical Journal*, 1955; 2: 867.

Fraser, I. 'The treatment of varicose veins.' *The Practitioner*, 1955; 175: 267–75.

'A visit to the USSR.' *The Practitioner*, 1957; 178: 98–105.

'Common injuries in children.' *The Medical Press*, 1957: 237.

'Advances in surgery.' *The Practitioner*, 1958; 181: 388–94.

'A propos de 96 tumeurs du grêle.' *Memoires de L'Académie de Chirurgie*, 1959; 85: 670–3.

'Four milestones in a century' [presidential address]. *British Medical Journal*, 1962; 2: 207–12.

'The discards of surgery.' *British Medical Journal*, 1963; 1: 839–43.

'Strangulated hernia.' *The Practitioner*, 1964; 192: 747–52.

'Great teachers of surgery in the past: Andrew Fullerton (1868–1934).' *British Journal of Surgery*, 1964; 51: 401–5.

'Progress in the treatment of appendicitis.' *Medicine Today*, 1967; 1, No. 5: 4–7.

'The John Snow Lecture. John Snow and his surgical friends.' *Anaesthesia*, 1968; 23: 501–14.

'Father and son – a tale of two cities.' *Ulster Medical Journal*, 1968; 37: 1–39.

'Dr MacCormac's report.' *St Thomas's Hospital Gazette*, 1968; 66, No. 3: 16–19.

'R.H. Hunter' [obituary]. *British Medical Journal*, 1970; 3: 290.

'The Mitchiner Memorial Lecture: The doctor's debt to the soldier.' *Journal of the Royal Army Medical Corps*, 1971; 118: 60–75.

'The doctor's debt to the soldier.' *Medicine Today*, 1972; 6: 32–5.

'The Campbell Heritage lives on.' *Ulster Medical Journal*, 1973; 42: 116–35.

'The Campbell Heritage lives on.' *Medicine Today*, 1973; 7: 110–33.

'J.M. Wilson' [obituary]. *British Medical Journal*, 1975; 1: 580.

'Safety in hospital.' *The Hospital and Health Services Review*, 1975, October: 1–6.

'The first three professors of surgery.' *Ulster Medical Journal*, 1976; 45: 12–46.

'The Sir Thomas and Lady Edith Dixon Lecture.' *Ulster Medical Journal*, 1977; 46: 103–4.

'Disease is good for you.' *Ulster Medical Journal*, 1978; 47: 141–50.

'The David Torrens Lecture. The training of a surgeon' [published privately]. 1979: 1–20.

Foreword to Odling-Smee, W. and Crockard, A. *Trauma Care*. London, 1981: pp. ix–x.

'F. Orban' [obituary]. *British Medical Journal*, 1981; 2: 678.

'The Belfast medical school and its surgeons.' *Ulster Medical Journal*, 1981; 50, supplement: 1–9.

'The Thomas Vicary Lecture. Sir William MacCormac and his times.' *Annals of the Royal College of Surgeons of England*, 1983; 65: 339–46.

'A guinea's worth.' *British Medical Journal*, 1983; 1: 707.

'Owlie.' *British Medical Journal*, 1983; 2: 1527.

'Penicillin: early trials in war casualties.' *British Medical Journal*, 1984; 2: 1723–5.

'He saw his own funeral.' *British Medical Journal*, 1985; 1: 1068.

'What would Hippocrates have done?' *British Medical Journal*, 1986; 2: 441.

'Bribery and corruption.' *British Medical Journal*, 1987; 1: 494.

'The personalities and problems of 60 years ago.' *Ulster Medical Journal*, 1987; 56, supplement: 15–30.

'Fernand Orban, 1902–81.' *Lives of the Fellows of the Royal College of Surgeons 1974–1982* (eds Cornelius, E.H. and Taylor, S.F.). London, 1988: pp. 304–5.

'The changing role of the physician.' *Ulster Medical Journal*, 1988; 57: 200–4.

Blood, Sweat, and Cheers. London, British Medical Journal, 1989.

'"Dickie" Hunter.' *Queen's Letter*, 1990: 8.

[Reminiscences of Professor W. St Clair Symmers] In *Pathology at the Royal: The First Hundred Years, 1890–1990.* Belfast, 1990: 33–4.

'Learning surgery in Paris.' *British Medical Journal*, 1992; 1: 1548–9.

Looking Back [published privately]. 1993.

'Random recollections of World War II.' *Ulster Medical Journal*, 1994; 63: 201–13.

Appendix 2

Honours

MEDALS AND DECORATIONS
By 1980 Sir Ian Fraser had accumulated eighteen medals and decorations:

one for gallantry – the Distinguished Service Order
six other war medals – the 1939–45 Star, the Africa Star with 8th Army clasp, the Italy
  Star, the France and Germany Star, the Defence Medal and the Victory Medal
two royal decorations – the OBE (1940) and the Knight Bachelor (1963)
two for work with the Association and Order of St John – Knight of Justice and the
  Order of St John Long Service (with three bars)
three royal medals – the King George V Jubilee Medal (1935), the King George VI
  Coronation Medal (1937) and the Queen Elizabeth II Coronation Medal (1953)
four foreign medals – the Belgian Ordre de la Couronne (1963), the Dutch Orde Van
  Oranje–Nassau (1969) and the French Ordre des Palmes Académiques (1970) and
  Légion d'Honneur (1980).

ACADEMIC HONOURS
Doctor of Science, Oxford University, 1963
Fellowship of the Royal College of Physicians and Surgeons of Glasgow, 1971
Fellowship of the Royal College of Surgeons of Edinburgh, 1976
Fellowship of the Royal College of Physicians of Ireland, 1977
Doctor of Science, New University of Ulster, 1977
Doctor of Laws, Queen's University of Belfast, 1992

Sources and references

Chapter 1

Published

Babington, T.H. and Cuthbert, A. 'Paralysis caused by working under compressed air in sinking foundations of Londonderry New Bridge.' *Dublin Journal of Medical Science*, 1865; 36: 312–18.

Burke's Landed Gentry of Great Britain and Ireland. Eighth edition, London, 1894.

Fisher, J.R. and Robb, J.H. *Royal Belfast Academical Institution: Centenary Volume, 1810–1910*. Belfast, 1913.

Fraser, I. 'The Campbell heritage lives on.' *Ulster Medical Journal*, 1973; 42: 116–35.
    Blood, Sweat and Cheers. London, British Medical Journal, 1989.

Unpublished

Fraser, James. Papers, including a manuscript note re his birth, his notebook, letter to Mrs Ellise (1854), books given to him (Boswell's *Life of Johnson*), Cuthbert family tree, Moore family tree, certificate of marriage, will.

Fraser, Robert Moore. Papers, including prizes from Ballater and RBAI, book given to him by Mr Henry O'Neill, certificates of marriage and death, will; ms account of a wedding in 1889; MD thesis (QUB Science Library q th20,D3).

Chapter 2

Published

Fraser, I. *Looking Back* [published privately, 1993].
    Blood, Sweat and Cheers. London, BMJ, 1989.
    'Random recollections of World War II.' *Ulster Medical Journal*, 1994; 63: 201–13.

Jamieson, J. *The History of the Royal Belfast Academical Institution*, 1810–1960. Belfast, 1959.

RBAI School News, 1914–18.

Unpublished

Fraser, I. Fuller text of 'Random recollections'; letters of application and testimonials for surgical posts in Royal Victoria Hospital; letters home from 1921 visit to Paris.

Chapter 3

Published

Anon. *Monthly Review, c.* 1935

Anon. *Ulster Medical Journal* 1939; 8: 133–7.

Calwell, H.G. *The Life and Times of a Voluntary Hospital*. Belfast, 1973.

Fraser, I. 'The International Society of Surgery.' *Ulster Medical Journal* 1939; 8: 46–7.
    'Great teachers of surgery in the past: Andrew Fullerton (1868–1934).' *British Journal of Surgery*, 1964; 51: 401–5.
    'The Campbell Heritage lives on.' *Ulster Medical Journal* 1973; 42: 116–35.
    Blood, Sweat and Cheers. London, BMJ, 1989.
    'Learning surgery in Paris.' *British Medical Journal* 1992; 1: 1548–9.

Looking Back [published privately, 1993].

'Random recollections of World War II.' *Ulster Medical Journal* 1994; 63: 201–13.

Froggatt, P. 'Sir Ian Fraser 1901–1999.' *Ulster Medical Journal* 1999; 68: 49–53.

Love, S.H.S. The Royal Belfast Hospital for Sick Children: A History 1948–1998. Belfast, Blackstaff Press, 1998.

Ulster Vintage Car Club and Moore, J.S. *The Ards T.T.* Belfast, 1978.

Unpublished

Fraser, I. Letters of application and testimonials for surgical posts in Royal Victoria Hospital, report on a visit to Vienna with the Surgical Travellers; talk on 'The bad old days – or were they?' (1983); letters home while on the Middlesex Hospital course and working in the St Helens Hospital; newspaper cuttings.

Fraser, Mark. Personal communication.

Chapter 4

Published

Fraser, I. *Blood, Sweat and Cheers.* London, BMJ, 1989.

'Random recollections of World War II.' *Ulster Medical Journal* 1994; 63: 201–13.

Reid, W. *Bush Proper 1941–1943.* Edinburgh, 1997.

Unpublished

Fraser, I ; diaries of Gold Coast posting; letters home from the Gold Coast.

Chapter 5

Published

Crew, F.A.E. *History of the Second World War: United Kingdom Medical Series. Vol. II, Campaigns: Hong Kong, Malaya, Ireland and the Faroes, Libya 1942–43, North-West Africa.* London, HMSO, 1957.

Crew, F.A.E. *History of the Second World War: United Kingdom Medical Series. Vol. III, Campaigns: Sicily, Italy, Greece 1944–45.* London, HMSO, 1959.

Doherty, R. and Truesdale, D. *Irish Winners of the Victoria Cross.* Dublin, 2000.

Fraser, I. 'Penicillin: early trials in war casualties.' *British Medical Journal* 1984; 2: 1723–5.

Blood, Sweat and Cheers. London, BMJ, 1989.

Unpublished

Fraser, I. Diary of voyage to North Africa; DSO citation and newspaper cuttings; manuscript notes on penicillin.

Fraser, Ian (patient). Letters to I.F. dated 3 October 1988 and 24 July 1993.

Chapter 6

Published

Fraser, I. *Blood, Sweat and Cheers.* London, BMJ, 1989.

'Random recollections of World War II.' *Ulster Medical Journal* 1994; 63: 201–13.

Unpublished

Zulch, Karl (patient), two letters to Colonel Crowdy dated 18 November 1948.

Chapter 7

Published

Fraser, I. *Blood, Sweat and Cheers.* London, BMJ, 1989.

'Random recollections of World War II.' *Ulster Medical Journal* 1994; 63: 201–13.

Unpublished

Fraser, I. Diary (incomplete) and papers of Indian posting.

Chapter 8

Published

Anon. [RVH alphabets.] *Ulster Medical Journal* 1993; 62: 87–92.

Anon. *Snakes Alive,* c. 1960.

Fraser, I. 'The heritage of the Royal Victoria Hospital.' *Ulster Medical Journal* 1952; 21: 114–29.

'The Campbell heritage lives on.' *Ulster Medical Journal* 1973; 42: 116–35.

The David Torrens Lecture. The training of a surgeon [published privately, 1979]: 1–20.

Blood, Sweat and Cheers. London, BMJ, 1989.

Love, S.H.S. *The Royal Belfast Hospital for Sick Children. A history 1948–1998.* Belfast, 1998.

Unpublished

Fraser, I. ms eulogy for Miss Molly Hudson; printed application for the chair of surgery.

Fraser, Mark. Personal communication.

Chapter 9

Published

Anon. British Medical Association Annual Meeting, Belfast, 19–27 July 1962. Programme. *British Medical Journal* Supplement 1962; 1: 283–92.

Anon. *Journal of the Royal College of Surgeons in Ireland* 1963; 1: 59 [Vasilievitch Petrovsky].

Anon. *Journal of the Royal College of Surgeons in Ireland* 1964; 1: 157 [Eric Husfeldt].

Anon. *Journal of the Royal College of Surgeons in Ireland* 1967; 3: 43 [Jan Nuboer].

Anon. *Journal of the Royal College of Surgeons in Ireland* 1968; 4: 33 [Frank Bergan].

Anon. *Journal of the Royal College of Surgeons in Ireland* 1968; 5: 67 [Orvan Swenson].

Anon. *Journal of the Royal College of Surgeons in Ireland* 1971: 6: 132 [Philip Sandblom].

Anon. *Journal of the Irish Colleges of Physicians and Surgeons* 1977; 6: 151–152 [Ola Knutrud].

Anon. *Journal of the Irish Colleges of Physicians and Surgeons* 1980; 10: 90–91 [Daoud Hanania].

Anon. *Journal of the Irish Colleges of Physicians and Surgeons* 1981; 11: 85–86 [Loyal Davis].

Anon. *Knights Bachelor, 1964–1965.* 24th edition, London, 1965.

Eakins, A. *The History of 253 (North Irish) Field Ambulance RAMC (Volunteers)* [published privately, 1998].

Fraser, I. 'A visit to the U.S.S.R.' *The Practitioner* 1957; 178: 98–105.

'Four milestones in a century' [Presidential address]. *British Medical Journal* 1962; 2: 207–12.

Blood, Sweat and Cheers. London, BMJ, 1989.

Gailey, I.B., Gillespie, W.F. and Hassett, J. *An Account of the Territorials in Northern Ireland 1947–1978* [published privately, 1979].

Marshall, R. *The Queen's University of Belfast Services Club, 1918–1968* [published privately, 1968].

Potter, J. *A Testimony of Courage: The Regimental History of the Ulster Defence Regiment.* Barnsley, 2001.

Unpublished

Fraser, I. Correspondence, notes and programmes about the Order of St John; newspaper cuttings; certificates of honours; correspondence and diaries about visits to Gold Coast, N. America and Russia; correspondence, notes, letters and programmes about the RCSI and BMA.

Chapter 10

Published

Boyd, J.S. *Behind a Surgeon's Mask* [published privately, 1995].

Boyd, J.S. 'A memorable event. The men from Kos.' *British Medical Journal* 1995; 1: 727.

Fraser, I. 'Four milestones in a century' [Presidential address]. *British Medical Journal* 1962; 2: 207–12.

'The discards of surgery.' *British Medical Journal* 1963; 1: 839–43.

'The John Snow Lecture. John Snow and his surgical friends.' *Anaesthesia* 1968; 23: 501–14.

'Father and son – a tale of two cities.' *Ulster Medical Journal* 1968; 37: 1–39.

'The Mitchiner Memorial Lecture: The doctor's debt to the soldier.' *Journal of the Royal Army Medical Corps* 1971; 118: 60–75.

'The Campbell heritage lives on.' *Ulster Medical Journal* 1973; 42: 116–35.

'Disease is good for you.' *Ulster Medical Journal* 1978; 47: 141–50.

The David Torrens Lecture. The training of a surgeon [published privately, 1979].

Froggatt, P. *David Smyth Torrens and Sir William Wilde: Two Irish Medical Polymaths* [published privately, 1985].

Sinclair, T. 'Strangulated hernia through the foramen of Winslow: operation: recovery.' *British Medical Journal* 1909; 1: 646–7.

Unpublished

Fraser, I. Text of Downe Hospital Bicentenary lecture; 'Medical advances since the time of Bishop Jeremy Taylor'; 'Treasures of the Ulster Medical Society' and 'The Bad Old Days – or were they?'.

Chapter 11

Black, E. *A Sesquicentenary Celebration: Art from the Queen's University Collection.* Belfast, 1995.

Index